**Careers in
Librarianship
and Information
Science**

Careers in Librarianship and Information Science

Second Edition

Neil Wenborn

Kogan Page

First published in 1980 by
Kogan Page Limited
120 Pentonville Road
London N1 9JN
Reprinted 1982
Second edition 1987

Copyright © Kogan Page 1980, 1987
New material © Neil Wenborn 1987

British Library Cataloguing in Publication Data

Wenborn, Neil
　Careers in librarianship and information
　science.—2nd ed.
　1. Library science—Vocational guidance—
　Great Britain　2. Information science—
　Vocational guidance—Great Britain
　I. Title
　020'.23'41　　Z682.2.G7

　ISBN 1-85091-359-5

Printed and bound in Great Britain at
The Camelot Press plc, Southampton

Contents

Introduction   7

Part 1

1. **Basic Training**   13
   Librarianship 13; Information Science 18;
   Archive Work 20

2. **Public Libraries**   22
   Work in a Public Library 23; The Different
   Departments 25; Mobile Library Services 30;
   Opportunities in Public Library Work 30;
   Working Hours 31; Vacancy Information 31;
   Salary Scales 32

3. **Academic Libraries**   33
   Work in an Academic Library 33; Opportunities
   in Academic Library Work 37; Working Hours 38;
   Vacancy Information 38; Salary Scales 39

4. **National Libraries**   40

5. **Special Libraries**   43
   Industrial and Commercial Libraries 44;
   Libraries of Professional Bodies 48; Government
   Department Libraries 48; Hospital Libraries 51;
   School Libraries 53

6. Archive Work · 54

The Work 54; The Employers 56; Opportunities
in Archive Work 58; Vacancy Information 59;
Salary Scales 59

Part 2

---

7. Courses and Qualifications in Librarianship and Information Science · 63

Entry requirements for Library Schools 63;
Courses in Librarianship 64; Courses in Information
Science 91

8. Archive Studies · 96

9. Important Addresses · 98

Introduction

Library and information work covers a wide variety of different jobs. Whether researching into the derivation of English place-names or trying to book a summer holiday, people will always need information, and it is the job of the librarian, the information scientist and the archivist to acquire and organise that information, and to make it available to those who need it.

This may mean helping a schoolboy to find the best books for his geography homework, or using computerised information retrieval systems to assist the research of a team of marine biologists. You might be working with one or two other staff at a rural branch of a county library, or you might be one of a team of specialists acquiring antiquarian books for the special collections of a university library.

Obviously, an interest in reading and in sources of information is vital in information work, but it is equally important to be able to get on well with people and to find satisfaction in helping them. After all, information is there to be used, and you must be able to understand and, as far as possible, to answer, the various demands of the people who need to use it. You will often have to think quickly, and must be able to leapfrog from one subject to another at a moment's notice. You will also need to be methodical and patient — many readers' enquiries may take a long time to answer, and there is always a lot of routine work to be done to keep any library, archive or information service running. A good memory is also a tremendous advantage in most areas of library and information work, and an orderly mind is essential.

It is worth remembering, too, that jobs in library and information services can often be physically very demanding. You may have to spend much of the time on your feet, and books have a habit of getting heavier towards the end of the day!

In addition to the personal qualities already mentioned, the exploitation of information requires a thorough knowledge of bibliographical and other retrieval aids, and professional training is now essential in almost every area of library and information work if you want to progress to senior positions.

Professional and Non-Professional Staff

There is a growing distinction between the types of work done by professional and non-professional staff in library and information services, and it is a distinction which is likely to become even more firmly established in the future. There is a great deal of routine work to be done in most areas of librarianship, and if you go into a library or information service straight from school you will have a large number of clerical and handling duties to perform. These may include returning books to the shelves, answering the readers' more routine enquiries, typing, updating the library's own records, making out new book orders, checking material for damage, labelling books, levying fines, etc.

Although this kind of work can offer a satisfying short-term career, you will find only limited opportunities for promotion and will certainly be unable to progress to the senior positions in the library, for which professional training is essential. If you lack the minimum educational requirements for admission to a university or polytechnic degree course (see Part 2) you will find it a long and difficult task to obtain professional qualifications in librarianship. Other qualifications are available, such as the City and Guilds of London Institute Library and Information Assistant's Certificate No 737 and the Business and Technician

Education Council (BTEC) National Award Scheme (see page 15 and Part 2), but these are not professional qualifications and will not in themselves enable you to obtain more senior posts. However, BTEC and, in Scotland, the Scottish Vocational Education Council (SCOTVEC) qualifications are recognised by some colleges as acceptable qualifications for entry and may therefore enable you to study for a first degree.

If you are still at school, then, and are seriously considering a long-term career in librarianship, you will need to obtain the A levels required for admission to a university or polytechnic course, either in librarianship or in another subject. If this course is in another subject you will then need to take one of the postgraduate courses in library and information work listed in Part 2. Further details of how to obtain professional qualifications in librarianship, information science and archive work are given in Chapter 1.

The professional functions in a library include the selection and purchasing of new material, cataloguing and classification, the implementation of reader services, staff organisation, monitoring and attempting to answer readers' needs, liaison with the relevant financing authorities and with potential and actual library users in order to build up the most useful and representative stocks, supervision of conservation, etc. Most postgraduate courses in librarianship therefore involve both administrative and bibliographical training, and place considerable emphasis on the practical nature of library work.

The information explosion of recent years has greatly increased the need for specialists (particularly in scientific and technical fields) who are also highly trained in the techniques and demands of information work, and a new profession, that of the information scientist, has arisen to answer this need. Information scientists are now employed extensively in special libraries and information units. They have to deal with a wide range of different materials, from books and periodicals to microforms and tape-recordings, and specialist knowledge is often required in the handling and exploitation of these if their full potential is to be realised. Again, the nature of the work involved requires that information scientists must not only be graduates but must also have a postgraduate qualification in information science.

It is similarly impossible to progress to positions of responsibility in archive work without a good degree and a postgraduate qualification.

Part 1 of this book gives information about the wide variety of fields in which librarians, archivists and information scientists can now find employment, while Part 2 gives details of the courses and qualifications available for training in librarianship, information science and archive work.

Part 1

Chapter 1
Basic Training

Librarianship

If you want to make library work your career, it is essential for you to study through one of the schools of librarianship listed in Part 2 of this book. Almost without exception, entrants to librarianship as a profession now study for a first degree or a postgraduate qualification either of the Council for National Academic Awards (CNAA) or of one of the universities.

In order to progress to senior posts in almost all libraries it is necessary to be a Chartered Librarian, and to become a Chartered Librarian you must have either a degree in librarianship or a postgraduate qualification in librarianship. The Library Association, the professional body for librarians, keeps a register of Chartered Librarians in two categories: Associate of the Library Association (ALA) and Fellow of the Library Association (FLA).

There are four routes to Associateship of the Library Association:

1. Candidates must complete one year's approved training after the end of their course and must have registered with the Association at the beginning of their training. They must also submit a professional development report.
2. Candidates must submit a professional development report covering a minimum of two years' post-course experience and must have been members of the Association for at least one year.
3. Candidates must have at least six years' experience on

completion of an approved course (full-time attendance on an approved course sometimes counting for one year of this) and must submit a professional development report covering the whole of this period.
4. Candidates must have at least five years' experience of professional work in a library or information service, be able to show a level of understanding and competence comparable to that of candidates who have completed an approved course of study, and must present evidence of having undergone continuing education through courses etc at a professional level. All this must be evident from their professional development report.

Fellowship of the Library Association can be gained after five years as an Associate by the submission of various kinds of work.

Further details of how to become a Chartered Librarian are available from the Library Association's Education Department, 7 Ridgmount Street, London WC1E 7AE.

How to Enter Librarianship

There are two main ways of entering librarianship. You can either go direct to a school of librarianship from university or from the sixth form; or you can take a non-professional post in a library (as a trainee librarian or library assistant) before going on to a school of librarianship.

FIRST DEGREES IN LIBRARIANSHIP

A list of the library schools offering first-degree courses in librarianship is given in Part 2. The minimum requirement for admission to a first-degree course is five GCE/GCSE passes (including two at A level) or five subjects, including English, (of which three must be higher grade) in the Scottish Certificate of Education. Different library schools require different subjects in order to ensure that their entrants are properly prepared for their courses of study, and some may prefer candidates to have had some practical experience of library work. Degree courses in librarianship are of three or four years' duration, and most can only be taken on a full-time basis.

BTEC NATIONAL AWARD
If you lack the educational qualifications needed for admission to a school of librarianship, you may still be eligible for the Business and Technician Education Council (BTEC) National Award in librarianship and information work, which is a two-year part-time course. BTEC awards are recognised by some colleges as an acceptable qualification for entry. The minimum entry requirements for BTEC National Awards are normally a BTEC First Certificate or Diploma or four GCSE passes.

SCOTVEC HIGHER NATIONAL CERTIFICATE
In Scotland the Scottish Vocational Education Council (SCOTVEC) Higher National Certificate (HNC) is also recognised by some colleges as an acceptable qualification for entry to higher education. There is an HNC in Library and Information Science, further details of which are given on page 84.

CGLI LIBRARY AND INFORMATION ASSISTANT'S CERTIFICATE
BTEC also recognises the City and Guilds of London Institute Library and Information Assistant's Certificate No 737 as equivalent to its minimum entry qualifications. The Library and Information Assistant's Certificate is available to non-professional library and information staff. It is a one-year part-time course, but does not enable you to go straight on to library school.

Both the BTEC National Award and the City and Guilds Library and Information Assistant's Certificate require their students to draw on their own working experience.

POSTGRADUATE QUALIFICATIONS IN LIBRARIANSHIP
If you already have a degree in another subject, but want to

pursue a career in librarianship, you will need to take a postgraduate course in library studies. These are available on both a full-time and part-time basis at the schools of librarianship listed in Part 2. The full-time courses generally last for one year. The entry requirements for a postgraduate course are normally a good degree and some practical experience of library work. In addition to these courses, a number of schools offer higher degrees in librarianship.

Pre-library school experience can be gained by taking a non-professional post in a library (information on how to find vacancies is listed at the end of each chapter on the different types of library service) or, in the case of academic libraries, by the SCONUL Trainee Scheme, details of which can be found on page 37 and in Part 2. In addition to advertised vacancies, many librarians will consider applications on spec. It is always worth checking with your careers officer or with the Library Association that a given library will provide acceptable pre-library school experience, and you should also make sure that the library concerned knows you are only there on a temporary basis.

PRACTICAL TRAINING
Most undergraduate and postgraduate courses in librarianship place considerable emphasis on the practical nature of the subject, but your real practical training will take place during the course of your day-to-day work as a trainee librarian. Some libraries run special recruitment and training schemes, although many of these have been suspended because of present economic difficulties. Short courses in specialised aspects of library work are also notified by the Library Association. You are strongly advised to join the Library Association as soon as you begin work in a library, in order to ensure that you have the necessary period of membership and approved service for ultimate admission to the Register of Chartered Librarians.

SOURCES OF FINANCIAL SUPPORT FOR TRAINING
In general, it is no longer possible to train to be a Chartered

Librarian while earning your living. In the present economic climate it is obviously unrealistic to expect libraries regularly to take on staff with a view to sending them to library school on full pay, although a limited (and ever-decreasing) number do still run such training schemes. There is no central clearing-house for these schemes, but the Library Association may be able to give you advice about them.

As already mentioned, however, the BTEC National Award in Library and Information Work and the CGLI Library and Information Assistant's Certificate No 737 are specially designed for those who are already employed in libraries and information services, since the courses require students to draw on their own practical experience of library work.

If you are hoping to take a first-degree course at one of the schools of librarianship you may be eligible for an award from your local education authority. Further details of undergraduate grants are to be found in the Department of Education and Science's leaflet *Grants to Students: a brief guide*. For Scottish students the Scottish Education Department produces a *Guide to Students' Allowances* and students in Northern Ireland should consult their Department of Education's booklet *Grants to Students*.

The main source of financial support for postgraduate training in librarianship in England and Wales is the Department of Education and Science which awards a certain number of bursaries every year. These are allocated on a strictly limited basis to individual library schools, through whom application for the award concerned should be made. There are always fewer awards than there are places, however, so there is no guarantee that the offer of a place will carry with it the offer of a DES bursary.

Candidates from Scotland or Northern Ireland should apply to their respective Departments of Education for equivalent awards, and residents of the Isle of Man and the Channel Islands should contact their respective local authorities.

Further details of all DES grants for postgraduate study

can be found in the Department's own publication *Postgraduate Awards for Librarianship and Information Science* or requested from the DES itself.

It may also be worth contacting your local Jobcentre to find out whether you are eligible for sponsorship for the course you are thinking of taking.

It is always worth remembering that financial support for training can be very difficult to obtain, and that, if you are really committed to a career in librarianship, you may have to consider financing yourself.

Information Science

Information science is now an almost exclusively graduate field. An information scientist is as much a user of libraries as an organiser of library materials. Special libraries (and particularly scientific and technical libraries) often employ information scientists to provide and evaluate information related to the interests of the establishment concerned. This means that, in addition to a thorough understanding of information retrieval techniques, an information scientist should ideally have a knowledge at least to graduate level of such subjects as science, technology, economics, commerce, management or social science, plus a reading knowledge of one or more foreign languages, and a postgraduate qualification in information science. Most information scientists will have experience of working with computers and communication systems.

Postgraduate courses in information science are available on both a full-time and part-time basis at the institutions listed in Part 2 (see page 92). The entry requirements for these courses are normally a good degree in a scientific subject and an acceptable period of practical experience in information work.

A first-degree course is also available at Leeds Polytechnic and there is a part-time course leading to a Diploma in Information at Trinity College Dublin. Details of the entry requirements for these courses are given in Part 2.

The Institute of Information Scientists

The Institute, which is the professional body for information scientists, has four grades of membership:

1. *Affiliate:* for those who are academically qualified but not yet sufficiently experienced to qualify for full membership, and those who are engaged in professional graduate level work but not qualified for other grades of membership.
2. *Student member:* for those who are undertaking a course of study leading to an academic qualification in information science.
3. *Member:* for those who have both professional qualifications and approved experience of information work.
4. *Fellow:* for Members who, after 10 years in information work, can satisfy the Institute that they have produced significant work or have provided distinguished service.

In addition to the postgraduate and undergraduate courses in information science, certain courses in librarianship also confer partial exemption from the period of practical experience required for membership of the Institute, if certain options within those courses are studied. Further details are given in Part 2. More information about all these courses can be obtained from the institutions concerned, or from the Institute of Information Scientists, 44 Museum Street, London WC1A 1LY.

PRACTICAL TRAINING

As in librarianship, practical training can only really be obtained in the course of everyday information work. However, short courses are run by the Library Association and by Aslib in specialised aspects of information work, such as work with patents, mechanisation in libraries, business information, etc. These courses are notified in the Institute's newsletter *Inform*, and further details are also available from the Library Association and in Aslib's various publications.

SOURCES OF FINANCIAL SUPPORT FOR TRAINING
The sources of financial support for training in information science are basically the same as those available to students of librarianship. Further information about grants is available from the Department of Education and Science or from the colleges running the courses.

Archive Work

Archive work, too, is now an almost exclusively graduate profession. Central government repositories such as the Public Record Office in London recruit directly through the Civil Service Commission, Alencon Link, Basingstoke, Hants RG21 1JB, and will provide in-service training for graduates with good honours degrees, but for all other appointments a postgraduate qualification in archive studies is virtually essential.

One-year postgraduate courses are available to suitably qualified candidates at the University of Liverpool, University College London, University College of Wales, Aberystwyth, University College of North Wales, Bangor, and University College, Dublin. Most entrants to archive work have a degree in history and a knowledge of Latin, but these are not normally obligatory qualifications for entry to the above courses. The minimum entry requirement is usually a good degree, but applicants are also encouraged to spend some time working in a record office. (Addresses of record offices can be found in *Record Repositories in Great Britain* which is published by HMSO.) Further details of the above courses are given in Part 2, and additional information can be obtained on request from the institutions concerned.

Competition for the limited number of places on these postgraduate courses is always intense. The courses (with the exception of University College, Dublin) operate a joint administrative scheme. You can obtain an application form from any one of the four schools and should then send it to the school of your first choice. If this school does not accept your application it will automatically send your form on to the other schools.

Sources of Financial Support for Training

A limited number of DES grants are available for postgraduate study in archive work (except at University College, Dublin), but competition is again very keen and you may have to consider financing yourself.

Chapter 2
Public Libraries

Public libraries are perhaps the best known area of the library service, but it is nonetheless easy to overlook the variety of work involved in their day-to-day operation and the variety of different types of public library which exist.

Public libraries exist to serve the needs of the community, both at work and at leisure, and the size and organisation of that service depend very much upon the type of community concerned. An urban library may serve a town of a few thousand inhabitants or a city of millions. It may be housed in a couple of rooms in a converted rectory or in a central purpose-built complex with several departments and a number of smaller branches serving different districts. You might be working with one or two other people and a small stock of material, or you might be part of a large staff, dealing with hundreds of enquiries from users every week and handling many different types of material, from books to maps and microfilm.

Since the reorganisation of local government in 1974 the library authorities in England and Wales have been:

1. London Boroughs
2. Metropolitan District Councils or their successors
3. Shire Counties
4. Welsh Boroughs

This means that county libraries are now the principal library authorities, and include a number of urban libraries which had previously existed as independent units. For example, the county systems now include cities as large as Bristol, Plymouth and Stoke-on-Trent.

Work in a Public Library

The number of graduates in public libraries, though still relatively small (compared, for example, with academic or special libraries), is rapidly increasing, and it is necessary to have a professional qualification in order to progress to senior positions.

In smaller public libraries there may be less distinction between the work done by professional and non-professional staff, and you may be required to turn your hand to anything at a moment's notice. In practice, though, this will probably mean that professional staff will have to do more of the routine and handling jobs rather than that non-professional staff will do more of the jobs that are normally reserved for senior librarians. Certainly you will still find your chances of promotion severely limited by a lack of professional qualifications.

Most libraries, however, employ a number of school-leavers, and many send members of their staff on short courses to learn more about certain areas of library work.

Acquiring Material

Obviously, a librarian is much more than a guardian of existing information. For a public library to fulfil its purpose it must keep up to date with the sort of publications that its users are likely to want. This will mean keeping abreast of publishers' catalogues, bibliographies and users' needs and being able to make a selection from the quantities of books, periodicals, gramophone records, cassettes, etc which are constantly being produced.

The acquisition of material in a public library is a professional function. Public libraries are financed by local authorities, which control the budget for expenditure on library materials, but it is usually the chief librarian who decides exactly how that money will be spent.

In addition to the actual purchase of books, periodicals, etc, acquisitions work also involves the study of users' needs and inter-library borrowing or other means of supplementing existing stock. It may not be worthwhile buying a book on the history of welding techniques if it can be borrowed from another library when required, but the latest detective novel may be in such demand that the library will need to have its own copy or copies.

Organising Material

Once the material has been bought it has to be arranged so that the reader can find and use it as easily and efficiently as possible. Before a new book can be put on the shelves it has to be included in the library's records, classified and catalogued.

Inclusion of a book in the library's own records is a fairly straightforward job and is known as 'accessioning'. Classification, on the other hand, is a complex procedure which requires specific training and is the work of a qualified librarian. The majority of public libraries employ the Dewey system of subject classification. Under this system all books on a certain subject are given a standard three-figure number (for example, 930 for ancient history). This not only ensures that books on similar subjects are grouped close to one another on the shelves, but also that books on the same subject in different libraries using the system have the same number. It will often be difficult to decide on the best classification for a book. For example, it may not be possible to tell immediately whether a book on the treasures of Pompeii should be classified as art history, archaeology or ancient history, and it may be necessary to read it through in order to find out.

Cataloguing is also a complex process and demands high standards of accuracy. There are different rules and systems for cataloguing, but they all aim to provide an accurate and comprehensive guide to the holdings of the library concerned. Most public libraries have a catalogue arranged alphabetically by author's name and a subject catalogue, and these may be compiled on cards or in a file, or even, in an increasing number of cases, on microfilm. Accurate cross-referencing is necessary to give the reader as comprehensive an indication as possible of the information available. For example, our book on the treasures of Pompeii may be on the art history shelves, but a reader whose interest is in archaeology should be made aware of its existence from the catalogue.

Making the Material Available

The purpose of classification and cataloguing is to give the reader easy access to the information he or she requires. Obviously, the acquisition of material would be a futile pursuit if that material were merely left on the shelves and never used. Reader services represent one of the most important aspects of the librarian's work.

In a public library many of the readers' needs are likely to be recreational, but the librarian must nonetheless be fully conversant with the bibliographical tools of the trade. Most librarians also provide reference services for readers, and many public libraries mount exhibitions to bring certain areas of the library's stock or of the life of the community to readers' attention.

The Different Departments

Public libraries are generally divided into sections offering different services to different classes of readers or answering different reader needs. In the smaller libraries these sections (reference section, children's library, etc) may well be housed in different parts of the same room, and you may need to turn your hand to whichever is busiest at any given time. In larger libraries, however, the different departments will probably be housed separately, with permanent staff attached specifically to each. In recent years many public libraries have been expanding their service to include loans of records, cassettes, compact discs and even reproductions of pictures, and there is an increasing need for staff who have been trained to understand the special problems of storage and conservation which this sort of material raises. Other libraries have become not only 'resource centres' but also cultural centres of community life, offering concerts, lectures, films etc as part of their service. In areas with large ethnic minorities, for example, the public library may provide an important link with traditional languages, literature, music, etc.

The Lending Department

This is usually the most extensive and busiest of the departments in a public library. The work of recording loans, processing returned books and replacing them on the shelves is usually done by library assistants who are unqualified staff, but, especially in smaller public libraries, the professional staff too may sometimes have to take their turn at the more routine jobs. There is a lot of routine work to be done, but one of the major compensations is the contact with the public which information work demands. Nowhere is this more true than in the lending department of a public library. One minute you may be helping an old lady to find the novel she wants in a large print edition; the next minute you may be trying to trace a book on brass rubbing for someone who is following up an evening class reading list. You will meet a wide range of people with a correspondingly wide range of interests, and you may well be asked to help find information on the most unusual subjects. You will also grow to recognise the needs of your regular users.

There will, of course, be the 'awkward customers' who expect you to know everything there is to know about whatever subject they are interested in, or people who have lost their tickets or library books. Not only will you need a thorough knowledge of the library itself, you will also need a lot of patience and a lot of stamina. You will probably have to spend a large part of the average day on your feet.

The Children's Department

Many public libraries have a separate children's section, and some have an additional section for 'young adults'. These

Public Libraries

are services which raise special problems of selection and organisation, and may provide a challenging and rewarding working environment. Jan, a school-leaver who works in the children's department of a large public library, finds the job varied and interesting. She says: 'It can get very busy — especially on Saturdays. Lots of the children know exactly what they want and they expect you to be able to find it for them. Some of the others are very shy and you have to help and encourage them.' Many of the larger children's departments have close links with local schools and may lend material to school libraries in the area, as well as advising school librarians and teachers on the choice of reading material for their younger pupils. The children's librarian may arrange for classes from local schools to come along and be introduced to the library service, and may mount exhibitions of the work of children in the area.

Parents often use children's libraries in order to find suitable reading matter for their young sons and daughters, or to look for books to help the children with their homework. The children's librarian will play an influential role in the formation and direction of children's reading tastes and habits, and a policy for selection of appropriate and attractive material will have to be drawn up with care and discrimination. Day-to-day contact with children, some of whom may be vague about the workings of the library, demands a special degree of patience and understanding, and the ability to be helpful without appearing patronising.

You will also need to be firm on occasions. Most children will be well behaved and careful, but there is always the danger, especially with the very young, that books will be returned damaged or scribbled on. Again, an ability to deal with people, whether parents, teachers or the children themselves, is essential to the job.

The Music Department

Many public libraries now provide a gramophone record service, and some also loan tapes, cassettes and even compact discs, raising special problems of selection, storage and care. In some cases libraries impose restrictions upon the use of these materials and may require details of the equipment on which records or tapes are to be played. Excessive cartridge weight or a worn stylus can do permanent damage to a record, and even with careful handling both records and tapes are highly susceptible to wear and deterioration in quality. Stock will need to be regularly checked.

The actual loan procedure will vary from library to library, but it is likely to be similar to that operated in the main lending department. Most music departments also lend scores, and may have separate collections of musical biographies, bibliographies, etc. Whether or not staff are employed specifically to deal with the music section will obviously depend upon the size and organisation of the library in question. In some libraries staff may be involved in the organisation and administration of gramophone record recitals or concerts for users and members of the local community.

The Local History Department

The role of the public library as a cultural centre of community life has led to many libraries building up stocks of material relating to the local history of the area concerned, thus providing a valuable service for research. One such library, for example, has an extensive collection of ephemera relating to the history of its county, ranging from architectural plans to advertisements for village fetes. The local history librarian maintains close links with urban and rural authorities and local history societies, and sometimes conducts lectures on aspects of local history, as well as mounting exhibitions, both at the library and elsewhere, of photographs and documents of local historic interest. As with the archivist, part of the local history librarian's job is deciding what to preserve and what to reject from the mass of material produced in a specific area. Every parish newsletter, every playbill advertising a local production, has a potential claim to being the research material of the future. At the same time, of course, storage space is invariably at a premium in libraries and, even with developments in microfilm and microfiche, originals still have to be kept somewhere.

The Reference Department

Most public libraries have a separate reference section which will contain such basic reference tools as dictionaries, encyclopedias, bibliographies, directories and yearbooks. Whereas many of the enquiries in the lending department of a public library will be for works of fiction or other recreational books, work in a reference library is more likely to involve helping readers to find and use the information sources they require. As in all areas of library work, an interest in and knowledge of the *sources* of information, and the *means* of pinpointing and retrieving the information required, is as important as an interest in the publications themselves.

In addition to a thorough knowledge of the bibliographical and reference tools available (such as the British National Bibliography or the British Union Catalogue of Periodicals), you will also need to acquire a comprehensive working knowledge of the holdings of your particular reference library. Library school courses provide an extensive training in bibliographical searching, but the practical application of that training in the day-to-day work of a library may involve you in the use of considerable 'lateral thinking'. How, for example, would you help a reader find out about fluctuations in the Brazilian coffee crop? Again, some readers may wish you not just to point out the best source of information about the subject in which they are interested, but actually to provide them with specific facts. One of the fascinations of information work is the way in which one piece of information can lead on to others, in much the same way as looking up one word in a dictionary can lead you on to other definitions and cross references. It is extraordinary how helpful apparently 'useless' facts remembered from conversations or television programmes can sometimes be in suggesting new lines of enquiry for reader and librarian alike.

Most public libraries also provide reference copies of selected newspapers and periodicals, which are often housed in a separate reading room. Some libraries, too, have specific study areas and facilities for students, as well as a wide range of standard works in scientific or technical fields. The larger public libraries may even have their own technical or commercial sections, maintaining liaison with local companies, and may well have facilities for searching computerised databases worldwide.

Again, part of the reference librarian's work is likely to involve the preparation of reader guides to the library's contents and the mounting of exhibitions. In some of the larger libraries a knowledge of and ability to handle audiovisual materials and equipment is likely to be useful.

Mobile Library Services

A considerable number of county and urban authorities now operate mobile library services. These services undertake regular tours to rural or suburban areas, providing a means of tapping the resources of the whole library system for those who might otherwise be unable to take advantage of it.

Opportunities in Public Library Work

A post in a good public library can offer a valuable start to a career in library work and the variety of jobs involved in the day-to-day operation of the library system can provide a broad and useful base of experience. This is especially true of the less rigidly departmentalised libraries where a wide range of professional functions will need to be exercised. In some libraries there may be opportunities for specialisation after a few years, but this will obviously depend on the organisation of the library concerned.

In recent years restrictions in government spending have

hit public libraries severely. Both professional and non-professional posts have been affected, as well as book budgets and expenditure on improvement of library buildings and facilities. This has tended to reduce mobility and increase competition for posts that fall vacant. If you are intending to pursue a career in public librarianship, therefore, you must be prepared to be flexible about the areas of the country in which you will accept a job.

Certain senior specialist posts, such as music librarian or local history librarian, may require relevant academic qualifications, but personality and experience are likely to be equally important. Professional qualifications are vital if you want to progress to senior jobs.

Many professional and non-professional functions are common to different areas of library work, and mobility between public and other types of library service is not uncommon.

Working Hours

Most public libraries stay open at least four evenings of the week and on Saturdays, enabling readers who work regular hours to have an opportunity of using their service. At present public library staff work 36 hours per week in the Metropolitan Police District and 37 elsewhere. Most have at least one day off each week, and evening duties are usually divided on an equitable basis. A rota is normally drawn up for Saturday duty.

Vacancy Information

Vacancy notices for public libraries appear in *The Times Educational Supplement*, *The Times Higher Education Supplement* and *The Times Literary Supplement*, as well as in other daily national and local papers. Advertisements for posts also appear in the *Library Association Record*, the fortnightly *Library Association Vacancies Supplement*, the *Municipal Journal*, *Opportunities* and professional journals in related fields. Careers service vacancy lists also contain vacancy notifications.

Salary Scales

Details of salary scales for librarians in local government can be obtained on request from the Library Association, 7 Ridgmount Street, London WC1E 7AE.

Chapter 3
Academic Libraries

Libraries in universities, polytechnics and colleges of higher and further education exist primarily to serve the needs of research and instruction. They provide material not only for undergraduates to use in their courses of study, but also for postgraduate research students and academic teaching staff to use in the pursuit of their research. To ensure that these needs are adequately met, senior members of an academic library staff must maintain close liaison with the academic teaching staff, and must be able to discuss with them at their own intellectual level the best means of fulfilling the library's resource potential. To progress to a senior post in an academic library, therefore, it is necessary to possess not only a professional qualification in librarianship, but also a good degree.

Work in an Academic Library

Much of the basic work in librarianship is common to all types of library. The processes of accessioning, classifying and cataloguing material, for example, are very similar to those in a public library (as described in the previous chapter), and the work of non-professional staff, too, is likely to be much the same and to demand comparable personal qualities.

Obviously, though, there are also a number of differences, resulting largely from the different nature of the material housed in the library and the different ways it is used. For example, in a public library (and particularly in the lending department) a large number of readers' enquiries will concern works of fiction or other recreational publications. In an academic library, on the other hand, fiction represents only a small proportion of the total stock, and demand for it is likely to be limited to students and teachers of English, classics, modern languages, etc. The majority of readers will be more concerned with works of non-fiction, and library acquisitions policy will also have to take account of the fact that much of the material required may be in the form of specialist periodicals and journals.

Again, a large part of the stock of an academic library will consist of works in foreign languages, and potential candidates for both professional and non-professional posts are likely to be at an advantage if they have language qualifications. For example, you are more likely to get a job as a library assistant in a foreign accessions department if you have GCSEs or A levels or equivalent in French, German or other modern languages. Similarly, a graduate in oriental languages may be invaluable to the oriental department. Books in a variety of languages, from Welsh to Serbo-Croat, will need to be classified and catalogued, and language specialists will therefore have an important role to play in the day-to-day operation of an academic library.

The work of library assistants in academic libraries is largely of a clerical nature and may involve such aspects of library routine as typing book and periodical orders, filing details of new accessions, manning staff desks in reading rooms, fetching and replacing books in the stacks or on the open shelves (not all academic libraries allow readers to borrow books), tracing missing material, etc. There are normally two or three grades of library assistant employed in academic libraries. Recruitment to the lowest grade is usually straight from school with passes at GCSE or A level or equivalent, and recruitment to the higher grades is either by promotion or from library assistants who have gained experience in other libraries.

Senior posts are in almost all cases closed to non-graduates and this may lead to frustration. Erica, 19, a Grade 2 library assistant in the accessions department of a university library, says:

> The work can be interesting, and certainly satisfies my liking for order, but it can also be repetitive. It's difficult to see where I go from here. Promotion within the department is unlikely at the moment, although I could move to a different section; on the whole I find myself taking on more duties, but without any increase in my actual status.

Senior duties vary according to the organisation of the library concerned and according to the department within that library, so it is impossible to describe a 'typical' senior post. The work of a senior assistant librarian in, for example, the antiquarian books department of a university library will obviously differ considerably from that of a comparably senior member of staff in a reading room. It is, however, worth mentioning the two most common types of organisation that exist in academic libraries.

Libraries Organised on a Subject Specialist Basis

In libraries of this kind each senior librarian is assigned to a specific academic subject or group of subjects, and takes responsibility for most of those aspects of the library's operation which relate to that specialism. He or she will be responsible for the selection of books and periodicals and for ensuring that the stock is kept up to date. The librarian must keep close contact with the academic staff of the relevant department in the university or polytechnic, and will have to deal with specialist reader enquiries. There may also be opportunities for giving seminars on bibliographical aspects of the specialist subject concerned, and some libraries may encourage staff to pursue their own researches by conferring study leave.

The majority of graduate applicants for academic library posts have degrees in arts subjects, and there is always a shortage of scientifically qualified candidates. Indeed, in general, candidates with unusual specialist subjects (within reason, of course) are likely to be in greater demand than graduates in, for example, English or history. Again, it is not always possible for an arts graduate to be given responsibility for a section which corresponds exactly with his or her academic specialism.

Libraries Organised on a Functional Basis

Here a senior librarian will be given responsibility for a department dealing with a certain aspect of the library system, such as cataloguing, accessions, reader services or special collections. At the same time, of course, he or she will find plenty of opportunities to make use of specialist knowledge.

For example, a reader recently telephoned a university library to ask if one of the reading room staff could try to find out how white and red wine was made to flow in separate streams through the public fountain when Charles I rode into the city of Oxford. Obviously, a knowledge of the standard historical works on the period concerned was an invaluable starting point for the librarian who set about finding the answer. (In this particular case, a knowledge of plumbing might have been an even greater help!)

Whatever the organisation of the library, senior staff are likely also to be involved in demonstrating the workings of the library system, either in person or by audio-visual presentations, to users, potential users, and visitors.

AN ASSISTANT LIBRARIAN DESCRIBES HIS WORK

It would be impossible to give an example of a 'typical' job in an academic library. However, an assistant librarian who works in the reading room of a large university library writes this about his job:

> My duties involve supervising a team of seven in the maintenance of the reading room copy of the general catalogue, and invigilating at the main desk in the reading room. This last activity takes up the majority of my time, and involves helping readers to use the catalogues and assisting them in finding information from reference books in the reading room itself. Locating books in a large catalogue has its own special problems, but the detective work involved is in itself fascinating, and there is considerable satisfaction in finding an obscure work for a reader. The great resources of the

Academic Libraries

library give one every incentive to pursue enquiries through a wide range of reference books, with a good chance of eventually being able to find what the reader requires. I also deal with some of the various enquiries which come to the library by post. The correspondents range from members of the public pursuing leisure-time interests to scholars requiring specialist information. There are also a considerable number of enquiries by telephone from members of the public, other libraries and, particularly, from newspapers and television companies. The main desk in this reading room is one of the busiest areas of the library, but working there is both stimulating and rewarding.

Opportunities in Academic Library Work

As in other areas of library work, senior positions in academic libraries are few in number, and financial cutbacks in recent years have still further reduced job mobility. Nonetheless, there is an increasing need for librarians with scientific backgrounds or qualifications in law and the social sciences, and the growing emphasis on information work and the use of computerised systems in academic libraries has also created opportunities for information scientists.

A professional qualification is necessary for appointment to intermediate and senior positions. Your first professional post may well be that of assistant librarian or senior library assistant, which is an intermediate post and involves duties which, though professional, are not strictly academic. Promotion from intermediate to senior posts is not automatic and to advance to more senior levels you may well have to move from library to library.

If you are a graduate and are intending to pursue a career in academic librarianship, SCONUL (The Standing Conference of National and University Libraries) offers a trainee scheme under which you can work for a year in an academic library in order to gain the practical experience required for admission to a course of postgraduate study at a library school. Posts under this scheme are salaried and competition for them is always intense. Further details of the SCONUL Trainee Scheme can be found in Part 2, but at the time of writing the entire scheme is under review.

SCONUL also arranges courses for academic librarians to study specialised aspects of their profession, such as the history and practice of bookbinding, historical bibliography, the use of computers in libraries, etc.

Libraries may also encourage their staff to pursue their own research, and some may offer study leave and opportunities for publication. Research is likely to be into subjects of a bibliographical nature, and it would obviously be a mistake to enter academic librarianship merely as a means of continuing your own research into other fields.

Non-graduate library assistants will find it virtually impossible to progress to senior positions, but those with appropriate academic qualifications may be encouraged to study for a degree in their spare time. The City and Guilds of London Institute Library and Information Assistant's Certificate No 737 is available by part-time study and the Business and Technician Education Council (BTEC) National Award is also available to non-professional library staff who meet the minimum entry requirements. Further details of both these courses are given in Part 2.

Working Hours

Working hours and conditions of employment vary from library to library and sometimes from department to department within a single library. Normally, though, you will have to do some evening and Saturday duties, which will in most cases be arranged on a rota basis.

Vacancy Information

Vacancies in academic libraries are notified in *The Times Educational Supplement*, *The Times Higher Education Supplement*, *The Times Literary Supplement*, the *Library Association Record* and the *Library Association Vacancies*

Supplement, as well as in national and local papers and professional journals. Careers services are also notified of some vacancies.

Salary Scales

Professional staff in academic libraries are normally paid on the lecturers' scale. The post of librarian commands the same status and income as that of a professor. Further details of salaries in academic library work are available on request from the Library Association or from SCONUL (see Important Addresses, page 98).

Chapter 4
National Libraries

National libraries in the UK differ in the size and structure of the services they offer, and the day-to-day work involved in those services will therefore vary considerably according to the nature of the library concerned.

Perhaps the most important of the national libraries in the UK are the British Library, the National Library of Scotland and the National Library of Wales. These are copyright libraries (as are the Bodleian Library at Oxford and the Cambridge University Library), which means that they are generally entitled to receive a copy of every book, periodical and newspaper published in Great Britain. In these libraries, therefore, the wide range of material available attracts a correspondingly wide range of users, from members of the public to scholars and television programme researchers. It also causes acute storage problems and heavy demands upon staff to keep catalogues and bibliographical guides accurate and up to date.

In most respects, however, the work involved in the large national libraries is similar to that in a large academic library, and the entry requirements too are comparable in most cases. A knowledge of languages, for example, is obviously a considerable asset at most levels. The National Libraries of Scotland and Wales both place emphasis on the literature of their own respective countries in their collections, and familiarity with such literature would therefore be an advantage if you were applying for a job at either of these institutions.

The British Library was established in its present form in 1973 to provide comprehensive reference, lending, bibliographical and related services on a national scale, and is divided into three main sections. The Reference Division and the Bibliographical Services Division are based in London and between them employ about three-quarters of the British Library's 2,000 or so staff. The Lending Division is based at Boston Spa in Yorkshire and provides a postal lending service to selected institutions. Work in this division is therefore likely to have a substantial administrative and organisational content.

The British Library is an independent body with its own board, but the terms and conditions of employment for professional staff are similar to those for civil servants, and posts are advertised through the Civil Service Commission.

The terms and conditions of employment for staff in libraries which form part of the national museums are also very similar to those for civil servants. The senior curatorial staff are designated keepers and assistant keepers, and their work may have a substantial administrative content. The work of a research assistant in a national museum library is roughly comparable to that of an assistant librarian in an academic library, and museum assistants perform duties similar to those of library assistants, replacing books on shelves, answering the more routine enquiries, etc.

In the more specialised national libraries, then, you would be dealing with a narrower range of readers and material than, for example, in the British Library Reference Division, but would need to have a greater in-depth knowledge of the subject area or areas concerned. The Science Museum Library and the Victoria and Albert Museum Library are examples, the latter housing one of the finest collections of the literature of art to be found anywhere in the world. In a specialist museum library a professional qualification in librarianship, although obviously a desirable advantage, may not be as essential as a specialist knowledge of the field concerned, preferably reflected in academic achievement or research experience. Again, it may be possible for museum assistants in some fields to progress to positions of greater responsibility than would normally be open to them in, for example, a university library, by virtue of specialist knowledge acquired either inside or outside the job. Staff mobility between museum and library is also a possibility.

Chapter 5
Special Libraries

Special libraries cover a wide range of information work and an equally wide range of working environments. In recent years employers in many different fields have come to realise the need for efficient information services in their respective organisations, and opportunities now exist for qualified librarians in areas as diverse as scientific research establishments, newspaper offices and hospitals. Government departments and government laboratories employ a large proportion of the professional librarians involved in special libraries and information units, as do learned societies and trade or research associations. The remainder are very largely in industry and commerce, and in this field the number of jobs available has been showing some increase in recent years. In all these areas the emphasis is on speedy and efficient information handling and retrieval rather than on the building up of stocks, and special libraries are therefore extensive employers of information scientists as well as of professional librarians.

As a special librarian you will need to have a thorough knowledge of the field in which you are employed, and must be able to understand, meet and, as far as possible, anticipate the requirements of your colleagues in the organisation where you work. It is therefore highly desirable that a special librarian or information officer should not only be a Chartered Librarian, but should also have a good degree in an appropriate discipline. Since much of the content of special libraries is likely to be of a technical nature, a degree or higher qualification in a scientific subject or in economics or the social sciences will often be required, although there is a limited number of jobs for which an arts degree is a more appropriate qualification. A knowledge of computerised information retrieval and communication systems is also becoming increasingly necessary.

Industrial and Commercial Libraries

Until recently, a number of industrial and commercial libraries were run on a 'caretaker' basis by a member of staff who had no specific qualification or training in information work. In some cases, these libraries were not supervised at all, and failed to serve the purpose for which they were originally set up. Nowadays, however, many organisations recognise the desirability of employing professionally qualified information officers in order to save both time and money by improving the efficiency with which information can be made available when and where it is required.

The job of the special librarian in industry or commerce is to provide an enquiry service for members of the organisation (or, in some cases, for people from outside the organisation such as students or research workers) and to keep colleagues up to date with information related to the company's interests. He or she must therefore build up a collection of materials (books, periodicals, pamphlets, standards, reports, patents, etc) which are relevant to the company's needs, and exploit this technical information to provide staff with a 'current awareness' service. This may take the form of direct personal service to members of the company staff (particularly where their functions and interests are clearly defined), or may involve the preparation and circulation of information bulletins or periodicals. The special librarian may also provide an abstracting or translation service for company staff, and a knowledge of foreign languages is therefore desirable.

It is also the job of the librarian or information officer in industry and commerce to store and organise the literature produced by the company itself. This may take the

Special Libraries

form of reports, memoranda, etc which may need to be found and referred to at very short notice by members of the staff. Librarians have a vital part to play in enhancing the efficiency of their companies, since their knowledge and organisation of the material concerned must be used to avoid unnecessary duplication of work and to make the accumulated knowledge of the company available to its own members. It is also the librarian's job to ensure that staff are aware of the library resources, which must be made available to every department in the organisation.

At the same time, the special librarian must be aware of relevant information sources outside the company, which means, of course, that he or she must be familiar with the holdings and operation of other forms of library service and with such bibliographical aids as are likely to be of importance to the company (such as, for example, the British Technology Index). In some cases these may need to be purchased and kept up to date in-house. The librarian should also, in the interests of efficiency, make sure that all members of the company staff know the range of the library's material and how to access it. He or she must also assess how best those resources can be used, which will require a wide knowledge of different types of information system and the ability to analyse, design and implement them.

Librarianship and information work in all its forms involves dealing with people and helping them to find and evaluate the information they require, and the librarian in an industrial or commercial environment must be as concerned with public relations as are the counter staff in a public library lending department. Furthermore, of course, as a special librarian in this field you would be providing a service primarily for your own colleagues, whom you will probably know personally. Consultation with them, together with your own specialist knowledge of the company's concerns, should enable you to anticipate and meet, quickly and accurately, the needs of their everyday work.

The work of non-professional staff in industrial and

Careers in Librarianship and Information Science

commercial libraries is likely to be similar to that of library assistants in the more specialised departments of an academic library. Even the more routine work, however, may require a knowledge of foreign languages and an ability to understand technical terms.

In some areas it is still possible for unqualified staff to progress to positions of responsibility as a result of specialist knowledge gained in the course of working experience, but the growing recognition by employers of the value of professional qualifications means that a library or information science qualification is likely to become increasingly important for promotion. However, opportunities for advancement within any one organisation may well be limited unless you are prepared to move into other areas of the company's business.

Case Study

An information manager describes her work.

> I work in a specialist technical library at the research centre of a multinational company in the energy field. The job requires flexibility and resourcefulness, since I act not only as the link between the on-site staff and the larger information community but also as a link with other branches of the company, exchanging information with them about company activities and providing them with regular reports.
>
> As information scientist I have to keep abreast of developments in information technology, including enhancements to various commercial on-line database command languages in order to conduct a wide range of searches for in-house staff. This in turn requires a sound knowledge of the range of research activities in progress at any one time. Building up a good relationship with on-site staff is an essential factor in being able to anticipate their information needs and make suitable provision for them. As librarian I am responsible for book and periodical acquisitions, ensuring that the journals reflect the changing research interests and that the reference section is catalogued and updated. I am also responsible for administering the library budget and ensuring that we acquire appropriate equipment, such as microfiche and microfilm readerprinters and desktop publishing software.
>
> My job differs from that of a librarian/information scientist in a large academic or public library in that I also have a

marketing/publicity role. In providing a repository for company information, the library has evolved into a producer of leaflets, technical brochures, training videos and other promotional material. I also liaise with the media and press, conduct guided tours for visitors and set up exhibitions.

Another important part of my job is to instruct on-site staff as to what services the library can offer, how they can use the resources provided and what they should look for.

All in all, the broad spectrum of the job makes it exciting and unpredictable, but by the same token it can be very hectic and is under-resourced in terms of staff. It has equipped me with specialist subject knowledge and has given me excellent experience in thinking on my feet and in being able to approach information problems in a creative way.

Training

Candidates for senior positions in industrial or commercial librarianship should normally be Chartered Librarians or have a qualification in information science. They should also usually have a degree in a scientific subject or in economics or the social sciences. In addition to this basic training, Aslib runs a number of short training courses in specialised aspects of information work.

Vacancy Information

Vacancies are advertised in periodicals such as the *New Scientist* and *The Times Literary Supplement*, as well as in the national press. Posts are also advertised in specialised journals and in *Aslib Information* and the *Library Association Record*. University careers services are also notified of some vacancies.

Aslib maintains a *Professional Staff Register* in which staff who are looking for employment or who want to change their job can enter their names and qualifications. Enquiries should be made to the Professional Staff Register, Aslib, 26-27 Boswell Street, London WC1N 3JZ.

Salary Scales

Salary scales for librarians in industry and commerce are

rare, but most employers review salaries every year and make appropriate increments.

Libraries of Professional Bodies

There are fewer openings in this field, but otherwise the majority of what has been said above also applies to professional libraries.

The precise nature of the work involved obviously varies according to the interests of the professional body concerned, but the basic function of the librarian or information officer will be the same: to acquire and organise relevant material, to provide an efficient enquiry service for those inside and outside the organisation, and to offer a current awareness service based upon up-to-date knowledge of the professional field.

Examples of professional bodies which employ librarians are the Institution of Electrical Engineers, The Chartered Insurance Institute and The Law Society.

Government Department Libraries

Government department libraries cover a wide range of information and users' needs, and vary immensely in size and facilities. Most departments have a large central library, and there are also a number of smaller libraries serving a variety of other establishments such as research and development laboratories. At one end of the scale there is the main library of the Department of Health and Social Security, which houses around 200,000 volumes and pamphlets and takes some 2,000 periodicals. The library produces current awareness bulletins, provides four abstracting services, and has a database available for on-line searching through two commercial host systems. At the other end of the scale there is the Fisheries Laboratory Library at Burnham-on-Crouch, which is a branch of the larger library at Lowestoft, serves the Ministry of Agriculture, Fisheries and Food, and employs a single librarian.

Obviously, the range of library work between these two extremes varies immensely, as do the subject fields with which, as a librarian in government service, you would need to be familiar. Government libraries exist primarily to serve the needs of their respective departments, but also provide a service to industry, to other libraries, and to members of the public who are researching into areas covered by their holdings. Most departments now make extensive use of computer facilities and databases, including international on-line facilities to Europe and the USA.

It would need a longer book than this to describe all the different types of work done by librarians and information scientists in government service. Here, however, is a list of the main departments which employ professional librarians. Further information about each of them can be obtained on request from the Establishment Officer at the address given below, or from the booklet *Librarians* in the HMSO *Civil Service Careers* series.

Government Departments Employing Professional Librarians:

Department of Employment Group
Caxton House, Tothill Street, London SW1H 9NF

Department of Health and Social Security
Alexander Fleming House, Elephant and Castle,
London SE1 6BY

Department of Trade and Industry
1 Victoria Street, London SW1H 0ET

Department of the Environment (joint library facilities with the Department of Transport)
Lambeth Bridge House, Albert Embankment,
London SE1 7SB

Home Office (joint library facilities with the Northern Ireland Office)
Abell House, John Islip Street, London SW1P 4LH

Ministry of Agriculture, Fisheries and Food
Victory House, Kingsway, London WC2B 6TU

Ministry of Defence
Lacon House, Theobalds Road, London WC1X 8RY

Scottish Office,
16 Waterloo Place, Edinburgh EH1 3BY

HM Treasury
Treasury Chambers, Parliament Street,
London SW1P 3AG

Training and Qualifications

To apply for a professional post in a government department library you must be an Associate of the Library Association or have an approved degree or diploma in librarianship obtained in the UK. You should also have some practical experience of library work. If you hope to obtain one of these qualifications in the near future it may be worth making a provisional application.

In addition to this basic training, government librarians are also sent on courses relevant to their fields of work at library schools and other training centres. Departmental training centres and the Civil Service College also hold short management courses.

Opportunities for Librarians in Government Service

Given the variety of work involved in different government department libraries, it is difficult to generalise about prospects for a qualified librarian. Promotion is by merit and according to the needs of the work, but good assistant librarians can normally expect to be promoted to librarian, either in their own department or in another, at a fairly early stage in their careers, and will have good prospects of progressing to senior librarian and higher grades. There is also some mobility into general administration from government library work.

Senior posts are not normally open to unqualified staff.

Working Hours

Librarians in government service have the same working hours and terms of employment as other civil servants. These are normally a five-day week (41 hours in London and 42 hours elsewhere), although some departments have flexible working hours.

Vacancy Information

Professional posts are normally advertised in *The Times Literary Supplement*, the *Library Association Record*, or the *Library Association Vacancies Supplement*, and further details of vacancies can be obtained from the Civil Service Commission, Alencon Link, Basingstoke, Hants RG21 1JB.

Salary Scales

Salaries are paid on a scale and rise by annual increments. Promotion to a higher grade is not necessarily dependent upon reaching the maximum of a scale. Further information about salaries can be obtained from your careers adviser or from the Civil Service Commission at the address given above.

Hospital Libraries

An increasing number of hospitals are coming to recognise the desirability of employing professional librarians to set up or develop the full potential of their library services. These services should ideally answer the needs of both staff and patients, and should therefore provide attractive and recreational material as well as an information service for medical, nursing, paramedical, administrative and technical staff.

Staff Needs

The hospital librarian will have to answer requests for information on a number of different topics, some of which may be extremely urgent. For example, with the recent expansion in the development and use of medical drugs it may be imperative to have quick access to reference sources about the side effects of a given product. You will therefore need to have a thorough knowledge of the library stock and of external information sources, as well as a comprehensive awareness of the appropriate bibliographical aids. There can be few other fields of library work where the speedy answering of users' enquiries can be literally a matter of life or death.

You will also need to provide services for further study, since many of those holding intermediate posts in hospitals are in the process of studying for higher examinations or are engaged in medical research. Here again you will need to be familiar with external study sources and the holdings and organisations of other libraries.

You may also have to provide a current awareness service of some kind in order to keep staff up to date with information relating to their particular professional concerns.

Patient Needs

At any given time a hospital is likely to be caring for a wide cross-section of the community. For example, a single ward may contain a university student whose studies have been interrupted by a broken shoulder and a housewife with a fractured leg. You will also have to cater for patients who are disabled in some way that may prevent them from reading normally, or with children or geriatric patients. By assessing and providing for their varied needs you will be actively involved in speeding their recovery. The selection and provision of appropriate reading materials is a responsible and challenging job, and some hospitals now employ the services of a Chartered Librarian in order to ensure that the varied demands of their staff and patients are adequately and efficiently met.

Opportunities for Librarians in Hospital Services

Openings for professional librarians in hospital work are very limited. Many hospital libraries still employ unqualified staff to look after their library services, and in others the job may be done by one of the doctors. In the present economic climate it would clearly be unrealistic to expect all hospitals to aim for the full range of services described above.

Further details about the opportunities available to professional librarians in hospitals, as well as information about salary scales, can be obtained from the Library Association.

School Libraries

The majority of school libraries are still run by teachers, often with the help of senior pupils. There is a limited number of openings for qualified full-time librarians but these tend to be restricted to the larger schools where the libraries may well be resource centres for audio-visual as well as printed materials. School library work involves organisation of the library, advising pupils and staff on how to make the best use of the facilities offered and liaison with the appropriate department or departments of the local public library concerning the loan and use of materials.

You will need many of the qualities of a teacher to run a school library (not least of which will be an ability to maintain discipline), and a thorough grasp of the educational needs of a wide range of age-groups.

Further details of developments and opportunities in school library work can be obtained from the School Library Association, 29-31 George Street, Oxford OX1 2AY.

Chapter 6
Archive Work

Archive work is now an almost exclusively graduate profession, and a postgraduate qualification in archive administration is also virtually essential if you want to progress to a senior position.

A degree in history and a reading knowledge of Latin, though often a great advantage in archive work, are no longer obligatory for entry to all the university training courses in archive studies and there are increasing opportunities for scientifically qualified archivists. Further details of archive training are given on page 20 and in Chapter 8.

The Work

The main work of the archivist is the preservation, safeguarding and organisation of the records of the past. The nature of these records may vary considerably according to age and use, and may include books, periodicals, loose papers, deeds, maps and in some cases tape-recordings, photographs and films. Documents may be in manuscript, print or typescript, and may be on paper or parchment or even wood. Their age may also vary considerably, from ten to a thousand years old.

Given the vast range of materials with which the archivist may have to deal, it is clear that his or her skills must include a knowledge of conservation techniques and of the particular forms of storage demanded by different types of records.

In addition, archivists must be well versed in the techniques of information work, since it is an integral part of their work to index and catalogue the materials in their charge, making access easier for potential users.

Indeed, the popular stereotype of the archivist as an introverted custodian of dusty papers completely overlooks the fact that archive work, in common with other forms of information service, has as much to do with people as with books and documents. In addition to providing reference and bibliographical guides to the materials in their care, most archivists also answer enquiries from members of the public, administrative bodies or the media, and may personally help enquirers to find their way around the materials in their charge. Many archivists also produce teaching material from their archives, and mount exhibitions or give lectures to make known the range and nature of the records available.

These educational functions are of particular importance because archives are not available for borrowing and if, as is usually the case, they contain unique and irreplaceable material, users may not even be allowed access to them.

Another important function of the archivist is the selection and preservation of potentially valuable records from the mass of documentation which is constantly being produced. Paradoxically, this may involve destruction of less valuable material in order to ensure that future generations of researchers are not faced with an unselective welter of paperwork.

As a professional archivist you need to be meticulous and methodical in your approach and must also be able to deal with people from a wide range of backgrounds and interest groups. You will also need the physical stamina to handle heavy and often dirty material and the discretion to work with sensitive records in absolute confidentiality. At more senior levels you will need to exhibit a wide range of administrative and management skills.

Case Study

Nicholas, 22, an assistant archivist in a county record office, regards his work as typical of that of a newly qualified archivist in local government. He writes:

> I am responsible for taking new accessions of material (which may be anything from a single document to 200 large boxes of documents) and sorting it into a logical order, numbering each item or bundle and producing a descriptive list of the material. I then index that list by place-name, subject and personal name. These accessions are phenomenally varied because county record offices handle documents from many different sources, including church records, borough and local government records (often going back to the Middle Ages), judicial records, private collections of estate records and personal correspondence, old title deeds, maps and plans, the records of local firms, and photographs.
>
> I also work in the reading room where members of the public consult our holdings, answering the questions of searchers, and being by turns a genealogist, a local historian and a legal historian. Answering postal enquiries involves dealing with a similar range of subjects.
>
> I select important documents for microfilming, identify documents in need of repair, give lectures on archives and related topics, and supervise classes held at the record office for groups of all ages.

He finds the work varied and stimulating, but adds:

> The archive profession is not one for the frustrated academic because in practice the archivist's time for assessment of the material he handles is very limited. One of his important responsibilities is to know enough to recognise the value of a document, but to leave it to others to make use of it.

The Employers

The majority of archivists in the UK still work in the public sector, and the majority of these in local government. However, there are a number of other areas open to the professional archivist and while opportunities here remain relatively limited they are generally increasing as more and more employers come to recognise the importance of efficient records management and maintenance.

The main categories of organisation which employ archivists are given below.

State Repositories

The main employers of archivists in the state sector are the Public Record Office in London, the Scottish Record Office in Edinburgh, the Public Record Office of Northern Ireland in Belfast, the British Library and the National Libraries of Scotland and Wales (see page 40). In addition, a few smaller national repositories, such as the House of Lords Record Office, offer similar opportunities, as do some specialist institutions such as the National Maritime Museum.

This is one of the very few areas of archive work where a professional postgraduate qualification is not essential. The central government repositories recruit through the Civil Service Commission, Alencon Link, Basingstoke, Hants RG21 1JB, and provide in-service training for graduates with good honours degrees.

As an archivist in the state sector you are likely to find yourself working as part of a larger team than would be the case in other areas of archive work, and you will find that promotion tends to take place within rather than between institutions. There may be opportunities to specialise at more senior levels.

Local Government

Most counties in England and Wales have a County Record Office or Archives Department, which may be either a separate department or part of the legal and administrative department. There are also record repositories in many district councils which are often closely linked to the local library service.

Local authority archives house a wide range of material, from ecclesiastical records to administrative correspondence, and the work of local authority archivists is correspondingly varied in its scope. It includes the collection, appraisal, cataloguing, storage, conservation and exhibition of records, and may also involve answering enquiries either in the public search room or by telephone or post, and giving talks and lectures to the public or at schools and colleges.

Promotion prospects are good, but you will have to be prepared to move from one part of the country to another as opportunities arise.

Industrial and Commercial Concerns

This is a growing area of employment for professional archivists, but one in which opportunities are still relatively limited. As with the special librarian in industry and commerce (see page 44), the business archivist is providing a service primarily for other employees of the organisation concerned or, in the case of professional bodies or trade associations, for their corporate or individual members.

It may prove difficult to advance in any one organisation without moving into other areas of the business or into more administrative work.

Universities and Other Institutions

There are a few openings for professional archivists in universities, often as part of the library or the history department, but opportunities are generally very limited. Archivists are also employed by a wide range of private and charitable bodies, but while the records in such organisations can be very absorbing and can provide an opportunity to immerse yourself thoroughly in a particular collection, there are very few posts in total and some of these will be on a temporary or fixed contract basis.

Opportunities in Archive Work

Because of the specialised nature of the work involved, the number of professional archivists is relatively small and openings are necessarily limited. Although there is now a wider range of work available to archivists, the majority are still employed in local government, where recent cutbacks have severely limited recruitment. However, because places on professional training courses are also limited, most archivists can expect to find employment at the end of their training.

Vacancy Information

Advertisements for posts appear in *The Times Literary Supplement* and in the national press, and some may be notified to university careers services. Local authority posts are generally advertised through the Society of Archivists' job circulars.

Salary Scales

Salary scales for archivists in local government are comparable with those for qualified librarians in the public library service, and in central government service (eg the Public Record Office) are comparable with those for equivalent grades of staff in libraries which form part of the national museums. Further details of opportunities and salaries in archive work can be obtained on request from the Society of Archivists, Suffolk Record Office, County Hall, Ipswich IP4 2JS.

Part 2

Chapter 7
Courses and Qualifications in Librarianship and Information Science

Entry Requirements for Library Schools

The minimum requirement for admission to courses in colleges of higher education, polytechnics and universities is five GCE/GCSE passes (including two at A level), or five subjects, including English (of which three must be Higher grade), in the Scottish Certificate of Education. Different schools of librarianship call for different subjects in order to ensure that students are suitably prepared for their courses of study.

The minimum requirement for admission to postgraduate courses is an acceptable degree. What is acceptable will vary from college to college as to both subject and class of degree. In addition, most library schools require or prefer their entrants to have had some practical experience of library work, but the extent of the experience required varies from college to college. It is always worth getting in touch with the college concerned if you have any doubts about your eligibility.

Details of student grants and awards for training are given on page 17.

This section contains a list of courses approved by the Library Association. The courses are listed by location of library schools, this being the method of reference most commonly used by bodies such as the Library Association, careers services, etc. Thus, for example, Robert Gordon's Institute of Technology is listed under Aberdeen, the College of Librarianship Wales under Aberystwyth etc.

Further details of all the courses listed below are available on request from the library schools or institutions concerned.

Careers in Librarianship and Information Science

Courses in Librarianship

1. First Degree Courses in Librarianship

(a) UNIVERSITY DEGREES (FULL-TIME)

Aberystwyth
College of Librarianship Wales, University of Wales School of Librarianship and Information Studies, Aberystwyth, Dyfed SY23 3AS, Wales
0970 3181

BLib Joint Honours in Librarianship and one other approved subject
3 years

BLib Honours in Librarianship and a modern foreign language
4 years

Belfast
Department of Library and Information Studies, The Queen's University of Belfast, Belfast BT7 1NN, Northern Ireland
0232 245133

BLS general degree in Librarianship and one other arts subject
3 years

Glasgow
Department of Information Science, The University of Strathclyde, Livingstone Tower, 26 Richmond Street, Glasgow G1 1XH
041-552 4400

BA pass degree in Librarianship
3 years

BA Joint Honours Degree in Librarianship and one other subject
4 years
(At the time of writing proposals are being considered for a new undergraduate course in Information Science which may replace the existing BA in Librarianship by 1989.)

Loughborough
Department of Library and Information Studies, Loughborough University of Technology, Loughborough LE11 3TU
0509 263171 ext 5239

BA or BSc Honours DPS in Library Studies
4 years

BA or BSc Honours in Library Studies
3 years

BA or BSc Honours DPS in Library Studies and another subject
4 years

BA or BSc Honours in Library Studies and another subject
3 years

(b) COUNCIL FOR NATIONAL ACADEMIC AWARD DEGREES (FULL-TIME AND PART-TIME)

Aberdeen
School of Librarianship and Information Studies, Robert Gordon's Institute of Technology, Hilton Place, Aberdeen AB9 1FP
0224 42211

BA in Librarianship and Information Studies
3 years

Birmingham
Department of Librarianship and Information Studies, City of Birmingham Polytechnic, Perry Barr, Birmingham B42 2SU
021-356 6911 ext 308

BA Honours in Librarianship and Information Studies
4 years (sandwich course, the third year being spent in a library)

Brighton
Department of Library and Information Studies, Brighton Polytechnic, Falmer, Brighton BN1 9PH
0273 606622

BA Honours in Library and Information Studies
3 years

Leeds
Department of Library and Information Studies, Leeds Polytechnic, Leighton Hall, Beckett Park, Leeds LS6 3QS
0532 759061

BA and BA Honours in Librarianship
3 years full-time
3-6 years part-time

Liverpool
School of Librarianship and Information Studies, Liverpool Polytechnic, 79 Tithebarn Street, Liverpool L2 2ER
051-207 3581

BA Honours in Librarianship
3 years (or 5 years part-time)

London
School of Library and Information Studies, Ealing College of Higher Education, St Mary's Road, Ealing, London W5 5RF
01-579 4111

BA Honours in Library and Information Studies
3 years

School of Librarianship and Information Studies, The Polytechnic
of North London, Ladbroke House, 62-66 Highbury Grove,
London N5 2AD
01-607 2789

BA Honours in Librarianship and Information Studies
3 years

Manchester
Department of Library and Information Studies, Manchester
Polytechnic, All Saints Buildings, All Saints, Manchester M15 6BH
061-228 6171

BA Honours in Library and Information Studies
3 years

BA in Librarianship
3 years part-time for qualified librarians
5 years part-time for non-qualified librarians

BA Honours in Librarianship
4 years part-time for qualified librarians
6 years part-time for non-qualified librarians

Newcastle upon Tyne
Department of Librarianship and Information Studies, Newcastle
upon Tyne Polytechnic, Lipman Building, Sandyford Road,
Newcastle upon Tyne NE1 8ST
091-232 6002

BA Honours in Information and Library Studies
3 years (an optional fourth year is also available, conferring qualified
teacher status)

2. Postgraduate Courses in Librarianship

(a) HIGHER DEGREES (FULL-TIME)

Aberystwyth
College of Librarianship Wales, University of Wales School of
Librarianship and Information Studies, Aberystwyth, Dyfed
SY23 3AS
0970 3181

MLib (by research and thesis or by examined study and dissertation)
1 year

MLib in Management of Library and Information Services (by
distance learning)
2 years

Courses and Qualifications

MEd in Curriculum Studies: school librarianship (jointly with the University College of Wales Department of Education; by research and thesis or by examined study and dissertation)
1 year

MEd in Educational Technology (jointly with the University College of Wales Department of Education; by research and thesis or by examined study)
1 year

MA in Periodical Studies (by examination and dissertation)
1 year

PhD
3 years minimum (although candidates who already have the MLib may be exempted from the first year)

FLA
(The college offers facilities for Associates of the Library Association who wish to gain the FLA by thesis)

Belfast
Department of Library and Information Studies, The Queen's University of Belfast, Belfast BT7 1NN, Northern Ireland
0232 245133

MLS (Master of Library Studies) (by examination and dissertation; candidates must already have the Diploma or BLS of the university)

MA (by research and thesis)

MA in Information Studies (by examination; candidates should normally have a good honours degree and 5 years' professional experience)
1 year

PhD (by research and thesis)

Birmingham
Department of Librarianship and Information Studies, City of Birmingham Polytechnic, Perry Barr, Birmingham B42 2SU
021-356 6911 ext 308

MPhil research degree (CNAA)

FLA
(The college offers facilities for Associates of the Library Association who wish to gain the FLA by thesis)

Brighton
Department of Library and Information Studies, Brighton Polytechnic, Falmer, Brighton BN1 9PH
0273 606622

Careers in Librarianship and Information Science

MPhil in Librarianship (CNAA) (by thesis)
21 months minimum

PhD in Librarianship (CNAA) (by thesis)
33 months minimum

Glasgow
Department of Information Science, The University of Strathclyde, Livingstone Tower, 26 Richmond Street, Glasgow G1 1XH
041-552 4400

MSc in Information and Library Studies (by completion of the instructional Diploma course and dissertation)
1 year

PhD (by thesis)

Leeds
Department of Library and Information Studies, Leeds Polytechnic, Leighton Hall, Beckett Park, Leeds LS6 3QS
0532 759061

MA in Librarianship (CNAA) (by assessment based on course work)
1 year (Jan-Dec)

MPhil research degree (CNAA)

PhD research degree (CNAA) (candidates normally accepted only by transfer after successful start to MPhil)

London
School of Library and Information Studies, Ealing College of Higher Education, St Mary's Road, Ealing, London W5 5RF
01-579 4111

FLA
(The college offers supervision of studies leading to the Fellowship)

School of Librarianship and Information Studies, The Polytechnic of North London, Ladbroke House, 62-66 Highbury Grove, London N5 2AD
01-607 2879

MPhil research degree (CNAA)
1-4 years

PhD research degree (CNAA)
1-4 years

FLA
(The college offers research supervision to candidates who wish to gain the FLA)

School of Library, Archive and Information Studies, University College London, Gower Street, London WC1E 6BT
01-387 7050

Courses and Qualifications

MA in Library and Information Studies (by course work, examination and report)
1 year minimum

MPhil in Library and Information Studies (by thesis)
2 years minimum

PhD in Library and Information Studies (by thesis)
3 years minimum

Loughborough
Department of Library and Information Studies, Loughborough University of Technology, Loughborough LE11 3TU
0509 263171 ext 5239

MLS (Master of Library Studies) (by instruction and dissertation)
15 months

MA/MSc in Library and Information Studies (by instruction and dissertation)
1 year

MSc in Information Studies (by instruction and dissertation)
1 year

MA in School Librarianship (by instruction and dissertation)
1 year

MA/ALISE (Archive, Library and Information Studies and Education) (by examination, assessed course work and dissertation; particularly but not exclusively for experienced librarians from developing countries)
1 year

MA in Archives (by instruction and dissertation)

Manchester
Department of Library and Information Studies, Manchester Polytechnic, All Saints Buildings, All Saints, Manchester M15 6BH
061-228 6171

MPhil research degree (CNAA)

FLA
(The college offers supervision of Fellowship theses)

Sheffield
Department of Information Studies, University of Sheffield, Western Bank, Sheffield S10 2TN
0742 78555 ext 6012

MA in Librarianship (by assessment of course work and dissertation)
1 year

MSc in Information Studies (by assessment of course work and dissertation)
1 year

MA in Information Studies (Social Sciences) (by assessment of course work and dissertation)
1 year

MPhil (by thesis)

PhD (by thesis)

(b) HIGHER DEGREES (PART-TIME)

Aberystwyth
College of Librarianship Wales, University of Wales School of Librarianship and Information Studies, Aberystwyth, Dyfed SY23 3AS
0970 3181

MLib (by research and thesis)
2 years minimum (at least 3 months of which in total must be spent in residence)

PhD
5 years minimum (although candidates who already have the MLib may be exempted from the first year)

FLA
(The college offers facilities for Associates of the Library Association who wish to gain the FLA by thesis)

Belfast
Department of Library and Information Studies, The Queen's University of Belfast, Belfast BT7 1NN, Northern Ireland
0232 245133

MA in Information Studies (by examination; candidates should normally have a good honours degree and 5 years' professional experience)
2 years

Brighton
Department of Library and Information Studies, Brighton Polytechnic, Falmer, Brighton BN1 9PH
0273 606622

MPhil in Librarianship (CNAA) (by thesis)
33 months minimum

PhD in Librarianship (CNAA) (by thesis)
45 months minimum

Courses and Qualifications

Glasgow
Department of Information Science, The University of Strathclyde, Livingstone Tower, 26 Richmond Street, Glasgow G1 1XH
041-552 4400

MSc in Information and Library Studies (by completion of the instructional Diploma course and dissertation)
2 years

Leeds
Department of Library and Information Studies, Leeds Polytechnic, Leighton Hall, Beckett Park, Leeds LS6 3QS
0532 759061

MA in Librarianship (CNAA) (taught programme with assessment based on course work)
2 or 3 years

MPhil research degree (CNAA)

PhD research degree (CNAA) (candidates normally accepted only by transfer after successful start to MPhil)

Liverpool
School of Librarianship and Information Studies, Liverpool Polytechnic, 79 Tithebarn Street, Liverpool L2 2ER
051-207 3581

MPhil (CNAA) (by research and thesis)
33 months minimum

PhD (CNAA)
45 months minimum

London
School of Library and Information Studies, Ealing College of Higher Education, St Mary's Road, Ealing, London W5 5RF
01-579 4111

FLA
(The college offers supervision of studies leading to the Fellowship)

School of Librarianship and Information Studies, The Polytechnic of North London, Ladbroke House, 62-66 Highbury Grove, London N5 2AD
01-607 2789

MPhil research degree (CNAA)
3-5 years

PhD research degree (CNAA)
3-5 years

FLA
(The college offers research supervision to candidates who wish to gain the Fellowship)

School of Library, Archive and Information Studies, University College London, Gower Street, London WC1E 6BT
01-387 7050

MA in Library and Information Studies (by course work, examination and report)
2 years

MPhil in Library and Information Studies (by thesis)
4 years minimum

PhD in Library and Information Studies (by thesis)
6 years minimum

Loughborough
Department of Library and Information Studies, Loughborough University of Technology, Loughborough LE11 3TU
0509 268171 ext 5239

MLS (Master of Library Studies) (by instruction and dissertation)
3 years maximum (for British students only; overseas students are required to take the 15 month full-time course)

MA/MSc in Library and Information Studies (by instruction and dissertation)
2-3 years

MSc in Information Studies (by instruction and dissertation)
2-3 years

MA in School Librarianship (by instruction and dissertation)
33 months

Manchester
Department of Library and Information Studies, Manchester Polytechnic, All Saints, All Saints Buildings, Manchester M15 6BH
061-228 6171

MA Library Studies (CNAA)
2 years

MPhil research degree (CNAA)

FLA
(The college offers supervision of Fellowship theses)

Sheffield
Department of Information Studies, University of Sheffield, Western Bank, Sheffield S10 2TN
0742 78555 ext 6012

MA in Librarianship

MA in Information Studies

MA in Information Studies (Social Sciences)

MPhil (by thesis)

PhD (by thesis)

(c) POSTGRADUATE DIPLOMAS AND CERTIFICATES (FULL-TIME)

Aberdeen
School of Librarianship and Information Studies, Robert Gordon's Institute of Technology, Hilton Place, Aberdeen AB9 1FP
0224 42211

CNAA Postgraduate Diploma in Librarianship and Information Studies
1 year (Sept-July)

Priority given normally to candidates with practical experience

Aberystwyth
College of Librarianship Wales, University of Wales School of Librarianship and Information Studies, Aberystwyth, Dyfed SY23 3AS
0970 3181

DipLib (University of Wales Postgraduate Diploma in Librarianship)
1 year (Oct-June)

Practical experience preferred but not essential. Good honours graduates may register jointly for the MLib

Belfast
Department of Library and Information Studies, The Queen's University of Belfast, Belfast BT7 1NN, Northern Ireland
0232 245133

Postgraduate Diploma in Library and Information Studies
1 year (Oct-June)
Practical experience preferred

Birmingham
Department of Librarianship and Information Studies, City of Birmingham Polytechnic, Perry Barr, Birmingham B42 2SU
021-356 6911 ext 308

CNAA Postgraduate Diploma in Librarianship and Information Studies
1 year (Sept-June)
9 months' practical experience normally required

Careers in Librarianship and Information Science

Glasgow
Department of Information Science, The University of Strathclyde, Livingstone Tower, 26 Richmond Street, Glasgow G1 1XH
041-552 4400

Postgraduate Diploma in Information and Library Studies
1 year (Oct-June)
(Practical experience is not an entry requirement for the course)

Leeds
Department of Library and Information Studies, Leeds Polytechnic, Leighton Hall, Beckett Park, Leeds LS6 3QS
0532 759061

CNAA Postgraduate Diploma in Librarianship
1 year (Jan-Dec)
At least one year's practical experience essential

Liverpool
School of Librarianship and Information Studies, Liverpool Polytechnic, 79 Tithebarn Street, Liverpool L2 2ER
051-207 3581

CNAA Postgraduate Diploma in Librarianship and Information Studies
1 year (Oct-July)
One year's practical experience normally required

London
School of Library and Information Studies, Ealing College of Higher Education, St Mary's Road, Ealing, London W5 5RF
01-579 4111

CNAA Postgraduate Diploma in Library and Information Studies
1 year (Sept-July)

Practical experience preferred

School of Librarianship and Information Studies, The Polytechnic of North London, Ladbroke House, 62-66 Highbury Grove, London N5 2AD
01-607 2789

CNAA Postgraduate Diploma in Librarianship and Information Studies
1 year (Jan-Nov) for graduates with library experience
4 terms (Sept-Nov) for graduates without library experience
The preliminary term is spent in supervised work and study, but does not attract a DES bursary.

School of Library, Archive and Information Studies, University
College London, Gower Street, London WC1E 6BT
01-387 7050

Postgraduate Diploma in Library and Information Studies
1 year (Oct-June)

One year's practical experience normally required

Concurrent registration for the MA in Library and Information
Studies available to suitably qualified candidates.

Manchester
Department of Library and Information Studies, Manchester
Polytechnic, All Saints Buildings, All Saints, Manchester M15 6BH
061-228 6171

CNAA Postgraduate Diploma in Library and Information Studies
1 year (Jan-Dec)
At least 6 months' practical experience normally required

Newcastle upon Tyne
Department of Librarianship and Information Studies, Newcastle
upon Tyne Polytechnic, Lipman Building, Sandyford Road,
Newcastle upon Tyne NE1 8ST
091-232 6002

CNAA Postgraduate Diploma in Information and Library Studies
1 year (Sept-July)
Practical experience preferred but not essential

(d) POSTGRADUATE DIPLOMAS AND CERTIFICATES (PART-TIME)

Birmingham
Department of Librarianship and Information Studies, City of
Birmingham Polytechnic, Perry Barr, Birmingham B42 2SU
021-356 6911 ext 308

CNAA Postgraduate Diploma in Librarianship and Information
Studies
3 years
At least 9 months' practical experience normally required

Leeds
Department of Library and Information Studies, Leeds Polytechnic,
Leighton Hall, Beckett Park, Leeds LS6 3QS
0532 759061

CNAA Postgraduate Diploma in Librarianship
2-3 years

At least one year's practical experience essential

Liverpool

School of Librarianship and Information Studies, Liverpool Polytechnic, 79 Tithebarn Street, Liverpool L2 2ER
051-207 3581

CNAA Postgraduate Diploma in Librarianship and Information Studies
3 years

Students must be graduates employed in libraries or information work

London

School of Library and Information Studies, Ealing College of Higher Education, St Mary's Road, Ealing, London W5 5RF
01-579 4111

CNAA Postgraduate Diploma in Library and Information Studies
2 years

Practical experience preferred

School of Librarianship and Information Studies, The Polytechnic of North London, Ladbroke House, 62-66 Highbury Grove, London N5 2AD
01-607 2789

CNAA Postgraduate Diploma in Librarianship and Information Studies
2 years

Students must be in full-time library work

School of Archive, Library and Information Studies, University College London, Gower Street, London WC1E 6BT
01-387 7050

Postgraduate Diploma in Library and Information Studies
2 years

Students must be in full-time employment in libraries or information services

Manchester

Department of Library and Information Studies, Manchester Polytechnic, All Saints Buildings, All Saints, Manchester M15 6BH
061-228 6171

CNAA Postgraduate Diploma in Library and Information Studies
2 years

Students must be in full-time employment and are admitted in alternate years only

3. BTEC National Award: Double Option Module in Librarianship and Information Work

A number of colleges now offer this double option module, which is intended for those who hold non-professional posts in libraries and information services. It has been designed in cooperation with the Library Association.

The module is spread over two years and is organised on a part-time basis so that students can draw on their own work experience. Assessment is by two examinations (one at the end of each year) and two in-course assessments (one during the course of each year). If you have the City and Guilds Library and Information Assistant's Certificate No 737, the BTEC National Award may help you to progress to higher education even if you lack the educational qualifications normally required for admission to a library school. It is worth writing for details to the Business and Technician Education Council or your local college of further education.

ENTRY REQUIREMENTS

To register for a BTEC National Level course you must normally be at least 16 years of age, with a BTEC First Certificate or Diploma, four GCSE passes or a suitable alternative qualification such as a Certificate of Pre-vocational Education (CPVE).

The double option module in librarianship and information work aims:

- to provide you with an understanding of the nature and functions of different types of libraries and information services;
- to help you develop the ability to perform library routines, operations and services in respect of one type of library, according to the needs of the students and the employer;
- to provide you with an appreciation of the methods used by librarians and information scientists in organising and exploiting their services.

When you have completed the double option module you should:

1. Be aware of the purpose and function of different types of library and their inter-relationships, and be able to:

- outline the different types of library service;
- describe in detail, from your own experience, one type of library service (or section of a library) and its position in the general organisation;
- explain how different types of library are financed and outline major areas of expenditure.

2. Have a knowledge of the organisation, management and training of staff, and be able to:

- draw organisation charts for two different types of library;
- compare and contrast the functions of the staff included on these charts;
- distinguish between professional and non-professional work in libraries, giving examples from your charts;
- supervise non-professional staff, including associated technical, clerical and manual staff;
- prepare library staff records and keep them up to date;
- outline the major points of legislation concerning conditions of employment etc in libraries;
- explain the role of staff associations and trade unions in relation to library staff;
- describe the purpose of in-service training and suggest suitable methods for training staff included in one of your charts.

3. Have a knowledge of the basic materials required to operate a library effectively and of how to acquire these, and be able to:

- select at least two contrasting types of library and identify the basic materials required to operate these effectively;
- suggest sources for the materials you have selected and describe possible ways of acquiring them;

Courses and Qualifications

- explain the relevant library licence and discount arrangements;
- prepare materials for use in a library.

4. Understand the purpose of classification, cataloguing, indexing and filing, have a knowledge of the major schemes used, and be able to:

- explain these systems, including co-operative cataloguing systems, national, international and local systems, automated cataloguing and indexing systems;
- explain how an individual library can make the best use of these various systems.

5. Perform basic library routines, and be able to:

- compare and contrast the most usual issue systems;
- operate the issue system adopted by a particular library;
- explain and operate procedures for the registration of library users;
- explain the procedures involved in inter-library loans;
- explain the need for security in libraries and describe how the main security systems operate;
- describe the procedures for withdrawing and disposing of library materials;
- maintain simple accounts and records for such items as fines, photocopying, etc.

6. Make effective use of library materials, and be able to:

- list the principal categories of bibliographic record and indicate their range and use;
- describe methods of arranging bibliographies;
- demonstrate an awareness of the structure and range of the principal current English language bibliographies for books, periodicals and non-book media;
- demonstrate ability in bibliographic searching and in the compilation of booklists and bulletins;
- identify the different formats used in reference materials;
- explain, with examples, the uses of different information sources;
- demonstrate ability to use such source materials;

- explain the purpose and function of audio-visual equipment in libraries and be able to prepare and operate such materials and equipment;
- prepare and mount exhibitions using library materials.

7. *Understand the purpose and operation of services to users, and be able to:*

- identify services which any one type of library could provide for its users;
- explain the need for services to special categories of user, giving examples;
- demonstrate techniques for dealing with complaints from readers;
- describe routines and processes of inquiry techniques using illustrations from your own experience;
- explain the operation of SDI systems and perform the associated clerical operations.

8. *Understand the purposes, uses and production of library publications, and be able to:*

- describe different types of library publications and explain their purpose;
- describe stages in the production of these publications;
- demonstrate an ability to proofread these publications.

9. *Understand the purpose and function of library co-operation, and be able to:*

- describe in detail one scheme of formal library co-operation;
- outline the informal co-operative network of a library.

10. *Have a knowledge of methods of maintaining library materials, and be able to:*

- look after library materials and carry out simple repairs;
- describe procedures for binding library materials;
- explain the functions and purpose of equipment available in a library or resource centre you know;
- outline methods of shelving and storage for all materials, including the care of storage areas and the secure storage of rare, fragile and secret materials;

Courses and Qualifications

☐ demonstrate awareness of legal aspects of the use of materials, including copyrights, performing rights etc.

The BTEC double option module in Library and Information Work is available at the following colleges:

Bedfordshire
Dunstable College, Kingsway, Dunstable LU5 4HG
0582 696451

Cheshire
South Trafford College of Further Education, Manchester Road, West Timperley, Altrincham WA14 5PQ
061-962 2286

Stockport College of Technology, Wellington Road South, Stockport SK1 3UQ
061-480 7331

Cornwall
Cornwall College of Further and Higher Education, Redruth TR15 3RD
0209 712911

Devon
Plymouth College of Further Education, King's Road, Plymouth PL1 5QG
0752 264714

Hampshire
Eastleigh College of Further Education, Chestnut Avenue, Eastleigh SO5 5HT
0703 614444

Highbury College of Technology, Dovercourt Road, Cosham, Portsmouth PO6 2SA
0705 383131

Kent
Mid-Kent College of Higher and Further Education, Horsted, Maidstone Road, Chatham ME5 9UQ
0634 407391

Lancashire
Bolton Metropolitan College, Manchester Road, Bolton BL2 1ER
0204 31411

Tameside College of Technology, Beaufort Road, Ashton-under-Lyne OL6 6NX
061-330 6911

Careers in Librarianship and Information Science

Leicestershire
Loughborough Technical College, Radmoor, Loughborough
LE11 3BT
0509 215831

London
Brixton College, 56 Brixton Hill, London SW2 1QS
01-737 1166

Hammersmith and West London College, Gliddon Road, Barons
Court, London W14 9BL
01-741 1688

Southgate Technical College, High Street, Southgate, London
N14 6BS
01-886 6521

West Ham College, Welfare Road, Stratford, London E15 4HT
01-555 1422

Merseyside
Kirkby College of Further Education, Cherryfield Drive, Kirkby
L32 8SF
051-546 4078

Middlesex
Uxbridge Technical College, Park Road, Uxbridge UB8 1NQ
0895 30411

Nottinghamshire
South Nottinghamshire College of Further Education, Greythorn
Drive, West Bridgford, Nottingham NG2 7GA
0602 812125

Oxfordshire
Abingdon College of Further Education, Northcourt Road,
Abingdon OX14 1NA
0235 21585

Staffordshire
Cannock Chase Technical College, Stafford Road, Cannock
WS11 2AE
054 35 5811

Stafford College of Further Education, Earl Street, Stafford
ST16 2QR
0785 42361

Stoke-on-Trent Cauldon College of Further Education, Stoke Road,
Shelton, Stoke-on-Trent ST4 2DG
0782 29561

Courses and Qualifications

Suffolk
Suffolk College of Further and Higher Education, Rope Walk,
Ipswich IP4 1LT
0473 55885

Surrey
North East Surrey College of Technology, Reigate Road, Ewell
KT17 3DS
01-394 1731

Sussex
Lewes Technical College, Mountfield Road, Lewes, East Sussex
BN7 2XH
0273 476121

Teesside
Cleveland Technical College, Corporation Road, Redcar, Cleveland
TS10 1EZ
0642 473132

Kirby College of Further Education, Roman Road, Linthorpe,
Middlesbrough, Cleveland TS5 5PJ
0642 813706

Tyne and Wear
Newcastle College of Arts and Technology, Maple Terrace,
Newcastle upon Tyne NE4 7SA
091-273 8866

West Midlands
Bilston College of Further Education, Westfield Road, Bilston,
Wolverhampton WV14 6ER
0902 42871

Matthew Boulton Technical College, Sherlock Street, Birmingham
B5 7DB
021-440 2681

Yorkshire
Harrogate College of Arts and Technology, Hornbeam Park,
Hookstone Road, Harrogate, North Yorks HG2 8QT
0423 879466

Richmond College, Spinkhill Drive, Sheffield S13 8FD
0742 392621

Northern Ireland
Omagh Technical College, Omagh, County Tyrone BT79 7AH
0662 45433

The National and Local Government Officers Association (NALGO) also offers the course on a distance learning basis in conjunction with the Local Government Training Board (LGTB). Further details are available from NALGO, 1 Mabledon Place, London WC1H 9AJ.

4. SCOTVEC Higher National Certificate (HNC) in Library and Information Science

The Scottish Vocational Education Council (SCOTVEC) makes awards at three main levels: National Certificate (NC); Higher National Certificate (HNC); and Higher National Diploma (HND). Examinations for the advanced courses (HNC and HND) are held in December/January, March, May/June, August and October each year according to the requirements of individual courses.

The HNC in Library and Information Science is designed for technical support staff at sub-professional level in public, academic, industrial, commercial or governmental libraries. It covers the administration of the library and information department, information retrieval, storage and dissemination and reader services, and includes project work.

The SCOTVEC HNC Award is recognised by some colleges as an acceptable qualification for entry to higher education.

To study for the award you will normally need to have the former SCOTEC Certificate in Library and Information Studies or an appropriate programme of SCOTVEC National Certificate modules (further details of which are available from SCOTVEC at 38 Queen Street, Glasgow G1 3DY).

The HNC in Library and Information Science is run at the following colleges in Scotland:

Napier College, Colinton Road, Edinburgh EH10 5D7
031-447 7070

Telford College of Further Education, Crewe Toll,
Edinburgh EH4 2NZ
031-332 2491
(by open learning)

Courses and Qualifications

If you want to apply for entry to the course you should contact the college where you would like to study for it. Applications cannot be made to SCOTVEC itself.

5. City and Guilds of London Institute Library and Information Assistant's Certificate No 737

If you are employed in a non-professional post in a library or information service you may be eligible to take this one-year part-time course at one of the colleges listed on the next few pages. This scheme emphasises the practical nature of library work, and is designed to complement the training and work experience you are gaining in your own employment.

The course covers the purposes and functions of different types of libraries and information services, the main organisational routines associated with library operations and the in-service training of staff, the uses of the various materials and specialised equipment employed in libraries to answer bibliographical queries, and the maintenance, handling, storage and conservation of all types of library stock.

Assessment is by examinations, which are held twice a year. Further details of the Library and Information Assistant's Certificate No 737 are available from the City and Guilds of London Institute, 76 Portland Place, London W1N 4AA.

COLLEGES OFFERING COURSES IN CITY AND GUILDS
LIBRARY AND INFORMATION ASSISTANT'S CERTIFICATE
NO 737

Avon
Brunel Technical College, Ashley Down, Bristol BS7 9BU
0272 41241

Cambridgeshire
Cambridgeshire Libraries and Information Services, Princes Street, Huntingdon PE18 6NS

Huntingdon Technical College, California Road, Huntingdon
PE18 7BL
0480 52346/7

Careers in Librarianship and Information Science

Cheshire
Priestley Sixth Form College, Menin Avenue, Warrington WA4 6QJ
0925 33591

Cumbria
Barrow-in-Furness College of Further Education, Howard Street,
Barrow-in-Furness LA14 1LU
0229 25017

Carlisle Technical College, Victoria Place, Carlisle CA1 1HS
0228 24464

West Cumbria College, Park Lane, Workington CA14 2RW
0900 64331

Devon
North Devon College, Old Sticklepath Hill, Barnstaple EX31 2BQ
0271 45291

Dorset
Bournemouth and Poole College of Further Education, North Road,
Parkstone, Poole BH14 OLS
0202 747600

College of Further Education, Lansdowne, Bournemouth BH1 3JJ
0202 20844

Gloucestershire
Gloucester College of Arts and Technology, Brunswick Campus,
Brunswick Road, Gloucester GL1 1HU
0452 426504

Hampshire
Highbury Technical College, Dovercourt Road, Cosham, Portsmouth
PO6 2SA
0705 383131

Lancashire
Blackpool and Fylde College of Further and Higher Education,
Ashfield Road, Bispham, Blackpool FY2 0HB
0253 52352

Bolton Metropolitan College, Manchester Road, Bolton BL2 1ER
0204 31411

Lancaster and Morecambe College of Further Education,
Morecambe Road, Lancaster LA1 2TY
0524 66215

St John's College of Further Education, Lower Hardman Street,
Manchester M3 3FP
061-831 7091

Courses and Qualifications

London
Hammersmith and West London College, Gliddon Road, Barons Court, London W14 9BL
01-741 1688

Manchester, see *Lancashire*

Merseyside
Knowsley Central Tertiary Library, Rupert Road, Roby L36 9TD
051-489 1566

Mabel Fletcher Technical College, Sandown Road, Liverpool L15 4JB
051-733 7211

Southport College of Art and Technology, Mornington Road, Southport PR9 0TT
0704 42411

Northamptonshire
Tresham College, St Mary's Road, Kettering NN15 7BS
0536 85353

Nottinghamshire
South Nottinghamshire College of Further Education, Greythorn Drive, West Bridgford, Nottingham NG2 7GA
0602 812125

Oxfordshire
Oxford College of Further Education, Oxpens Road, Oxford OX1 1SA
0865 245871

Suffolk
West Suffolk College of Further Education, Out Risbygate, Bury St Edmunds IP33 3RL
0284 701301

Suffolk College of Higher and Further Education, Rope Walk, Ipswich IP4 1LY
0473 55858

Sussex
Lewes Technical College, Mountfield Road, Lewes, East Sussex BN7 2XH
0273 476121

Teesside
Teesside Polytechnic, Borough Road, Middlesbrough TS1 3BA
0642 218121

Tyne and Wear
College of Arts and Technology, Maple Terrace, Newcastle upon Tyne NE4 7SA
0632 738866

West Midlands
West Bromwich College of Commerce and Technology, Woden Road South, Wednesbury WS10 0PE
021-569 4590

Wulfrun College of Further Education, Paget Road, Wolverhampton WV6 0DU
0902 26512

Wiltshire
Salisbury College of Technology, Southampton Road, Salisbury SP1 2LW
0722 23711

The College, Regent Circus, Swindon SN1 1PT
0793 40131

Trowbridge Technical College, College Road, Trowbridge BA14 0ES
022 14 66241

Worcestershire
Evesham College of Further Education, Cheltenham Road, Evesham WR11 6LP
0386 41091

Yorkshire
Harrogate College of Arts and Technology, Haywra Crescent, Harrogate, North Yorks HG1 5BE
0423 55631

Huddersfield Technical College, New North Road, Huddersfield HD1 5NN
0484 536521

Richmond College of Further Education, Spinkhill Drive, Sheffield S13 8FD
0742 392621

York College of Arts and Technology, Dringhouses, York YO2 1UA
0904 704141

Wales
Ceredigian College of Further Education, Llanbadarn, Aberystwyth, Dyfed SY23 3BP
0970 4511

Bridgend College of Technology, Cowbridge Road, Bridgend, Mid Glamorgan CF31 3DF
0656 55588

Rumney College of Technology, Trowbridge Road, Rumney, Cardiff CF3 8XZ
0222 794226

Scotland
Aberdeen College of Commerce, Holborn Street, Aberdeen AB9 2YT
0224 572811

Telford College of Further Education, Crewe Toll, Edinburgh EH4 2NZ
031-332 2491

Northern Ireland
Ballymena Technical College, Farm Lodge Avenue, Ballymena, County Antrim BT43 7DJ
0266 2871

The Rupert Stanley College, Tower Street, Belfast BT5 4FH
0232 52111

Fermanagh College of Further Education, Enniskillen, County Fermanagh
0365 22431

Northwest College of Technology, Strand Road, Londonderry
0504 266711

6. The Standing Conference of National and University Libraries (SCONUL)

Most schools of librarianship require some practical experience of library work for admission to their postgraduate courses. The SCONUL Trainee Scheme offers graduates who intend to enter a library school, and who are UK or Irish citizens, a year's prior experience in an academic library. The scheme is run independently of the library schools, and acceptance as a trainee does not guarantee a place at a library school. The scheme runs from September to August, and the salary paid to the trainee varies from library to library. The number of SCONUL traineeships is very limited and competition is always intense.

Careers in Librarianship and Information Science

The aim of the scheme is to give graduates an overall view of the library system by supervised participation in the day-to-day work of an academic library. This work will cover a variety of duties.

At the time of writing, the entire SCONUL Trainee Scheme is under review. Further details are available from The Secretary, Standing Conference of National and University Libraries, 102 Euston Street, London NW1 2HA.

LIBRARIES OFFERING SUITABLE TEMPORARY POSTS OUTSIDE THE SCONUL TRAINEE SCHEME

In addition to the libraries participating in the SCONUL Trainee Scheme (a list of which is available from SCONUL at the address given above), the following institutions offer posts suitable for graduates wishing to gain pre-library school experience. Again, it is worth writing to the bodies concerned for further details.

Birmingham
The Library, University of Birmingham, PO Box 363, Edgbaston, Birmingham B16 2TT

Colchester
The Library, University of Essex, Colchester, Essex CO4 3SQ

Dublin
The Library, Trinity College, College Street, Dublin 2, Eire

Durham
The Library, University of Durham, Stockton Road, Durham DH1 3LY

Guildford
George Edwards Library, University of Surrey, Guildford GU2 5XH

Leeds
The University Library, Leeds LS2 9JT

London
British Library of Political and Economic Science, 10 Portugal Street, London WC2A 2HD

King's College London, Strand, London WC2R 2LS

University of London Library, Senate House, Malet Street, London WC1E 7HU

School of Slavonic and East European Studies, University of London, Malet Street, London WC1E 7HU

Westfield College, Kidderpore Avenue, London NW3 7ST

Oxford
Taylor Institution Library, St Giles', Oxford OX1 3NA
(A knowledge of two continental European languages is essential)

Some libraries and institutions, both within and outside the SCONUL Trainee Scheme, may prefer to take graduates from their own universities. Others may prefer candidates who have gained some experience of using libraries elsewhere. You may wish to find out the local feeling on this point before applying. It may even be worth writing to one of the previous year's successful candidates.

Courses in Information Science

The following courses are approved by the Institute of Information Scientists as fulfilling their criteria for information science, further details of which are available from the Institute. The courses confer partial exemption from the period of practical experience required for membership of the Institute.

Further details of all these courses are available from the colleges concerned.

1. First Degree Courses and Certificates in Information Science and Information Studies

Dublin
Trinity College, College Green, Dublin 2, Eire
0001 772941
Address for further enquiries: Dr M Sharp, Institute for Industrial Research and Standards, Ballymun Road, Dublin 9, Eire

Diploma in Information Studies
2 years (part-time, 2 evenings a week)
Entrants must have 5 passes in the Irish Leaving Certificate in matriculation subjects or A level equivalent or degree, and must have at least one year's experience of library, information or documentation work. The course is run in collaboration with the Institute for Industrial Research and Standards.
Exemption: 1 year

Careers in Librarianship and Information Science

Leeds
Department of Library and Information Studies, Leeds Polytechnic, Leighton Hall, Beckett Park, Leeds LS6 3QS
0532 759061

BSc and BSc Hons in Information Science (CNAA)
3 years (full-time)
Entrants must have the usual qualifications for admission to higher education.
Exemption: 3 years

2. Postgraduate Degrees and Diplomas in Information Science (Full-time and Part-time)

London
Department of Information Science, The City University, Northampton Square, London EC1V 0HB
01-253 4399

MSc in Information Science
1 year (full-time, Oct-Sept)
Practical experience preferred but not essential. The examination structure includes dissertation.
Exemption: 3 years

Postgraduate Diploma in Information Science
2 years (part-time, one day a week)
Students must be in relevant employment. Honours graduates who obtain the Diploma may convert it (within 3 years) to MSc by preparing a dissertation. An alternative programme is available to candidates with approved librarianship qualifications.
Exemption: 3 years

(MPhil and PhD in Information Science also available full-time and part-time.)

An Honours degree in a branch of science, engineering or economics is normally required for admission to these courses.

Sheffield
Postgraduate School of Librarianship and Information Science, University of Sheffield, Western Bank, Sheffield S10 2TN
0742 78555 ext 6012

MSc in Information Studies (Social Sciences)
1 year (full-time, Oct-Sept)
Entrants should have a good honours degree in Social Sciences or Law and approved work or research experience. Assessment by course work and dissertation.
Exemption: 3 years

MSc in Information Studies
1 year (full-time, Oct-Sept)
Entrants should have a good honours degree in science, technology or maths/statistics and approved work or research experience.
Assessment by course work and dissertation.
Exemption: 3 years

3. Courses in Librarianship Giving Partial Exemption from the Membership Requirements of the Institute of Information Scientists

Only students taking certain options in the courses listed below qualify for a period of exemption from the Institute's normal experience requirements for membership. The options required are listed in each case, together with the period of exemption which they confer. Further details of entry requirements, etc are given in the section dealing with postgraduate qualifications in librarianship. Additional information can, of course, be obtained from the institutions concerned.

Aberystwyth
College of Librarianship Wales, Llanbadarn Fawr, Aberystwyth, Dyfed SY23 3AS
0970 3181

DipLib (University of Wales Postgraduate Diploma in Librarianship)
1 year (Oct-June)

Options required in order to qualify for exemption: Information Management, Systems and Services, or Design of Computer-assisted Systems for Information Services.
Exemption: 1 year

Birmingham
Department of Librarianship and Information Studies, City of Birmingham Polytechnic, Perry Barr, Birmingham B42 2SU
021-356 6911 ext 308

CNAA Postgraduate Diploma in Librarianship and Information Studies
1 year (Sept-June) full-time
3 years part-time

Options required in order to qualify for exemption: Information Retrieval Studies, or Library Services and Materials for Science and Technology, or Library Services and Materials for Social Arts.
Exemption: 2 years

Glasgow
Department of Information Science, The University of Strathclyde, Livingstone Tower, 26 Richmond Street, Glasgow G1 1XH
041-552 4400

Postgraduate Diploma in Information and Library Studies
1 year (Oct-June)

Options required in order to qualify for exemption: Information Systems and Services, Management of Academic and Special Libraries; Bibliography: Science and Technology; Social Sciences.
Exemption: 2 years

Leeds
Department of Library and Information Studies, Leeds Polytechnic, Leighton Hall, Beckett Park, Leeds LS6 3QS
0532 759061

CNAA Postgraduate Diploma in Librarianship
1 year (Jan-Dec) full-time; 2-3 years part-time

Options required in order to qualify for exemption: Organisation and Management of Libraries and Information Units; Information and its Sources; Information Retrieval; Computer Studies

London
School of Librarianship and Information Studies, The Polytechnic of North London, Ladbroke House, 62-66 Highbury Grove, London N5 2AD
01-607 2789

CNAA Postgraduate Diploma in Librarianship and Information Studies
1 year (Jan-Nov) for graduates with library experience; 4 terms (Sept-Nov) for graduates without library experience; 2 years part-time

Options required in order to qualify for exemption: consult the Institute of Information Scientists for details
Exemption: 2 years

Loughborough
Department of Library and Information Studies, Loughborough University of Technology, Loughborough LE11 3TU
0509 263171 ext 5239

MSc in Information Studies
1 year full-time; 2-3 years part-time

Options required in order to qualify for exemption: either S5 Information Service Studies, or 2 from E2 Current Awareness

Services from Libraries, E3 Business Information, E4 Advanced Information, E8 Health Science
Exemption: consult the Institute of Information Scientists

Manchester
Department of Library and Information Studies, Manchester Polytechnic, All Saints Buildings, All Saints, Manchester M15 6BH
061-228 6171

CNAA Postgraduate Diploma in Library and Information Studies
1 year (Jan-Dec) full-time; 2 years part-time

Options required in order to qualify for exemption: consult the Institute of Information Scientists for details.
Exemption: 2 years

Chapter 8
Archive Studies

A postgraduate qualification is now almost essential if you intend to pursue a career in archive work. Postgraduate courses are available at the universities listed, and the minimum requirement for admission is normally a good honours degree in an arts subject. Some of the universities may prefer their candidates to have a degree in history, and for some options within the courses a knowledge of Latin may be necessary. There is also some scope for candidates with scientific or business studies training. Most universities prefer their candidates to have had some practical experience of work in a record office, even though practical work forms a part of the courses themselves. The content and emphasis of the courses vary and it is always worth writing for a prospectus before deciding on your choices.

It is also worth bearing in mind that there are few places on these courses and even fewer DES grants to finance participating students, and that competition for both is always fierce. You will have to demonstrate an *informed* interest in archive work, and this means that you should have at least looked round a record office and preferably have worked in one. The staff of record offices are normally willing to show prospective students around and to answer questions, so it is well worth writing to your nearest City or County Record Office to ask if you can arrange a visit.

Further details of training and admission procedures are given on page 20.

Aberystwyth
University College of Wales, Department of History, Hugh Owen Building, Aberystwyth, Dyfed SY23 3DY
0970 3111

Archive Studies

Diploma in Archive Administration
1 year (approval may be given to students undertaking research for a master's degree to spread the course over 2 years)

Bangor
University College of North Wales, Bangor, Gwynedd LL57 2DG
0248 351151

Diploma in Archive Administration
1 year

Dublin
University College Dublin, Archives Department, Belfield, Dublin 4
0001 693244

Diploma in Archival Studies
1 year

Liverpool
School of History, University of Liverpool, 8 Abercromby Square, PO Box 147, Liverpool L69 3BX
051-709 6022

Master's Degree in Archive Administration
1 year

London
School of Library, Archive and Information Studies, University College London, Gower Street, London WC1E 6BT
01-387 7050

Diploma in Archive Studies
1 year full-time (students are also accepted part-time)

Chapter 9

Important Addresses

Aslib
26-27 Boswell Street, London WC1N 3JZ
01-430 2671

Business Archives Council
15 Tooley Street, London SE1 2PN
01-407 6110

Business and Technician Education Council (BTEC)
Central House, Upper Woburn Place, London WC1H 0HH
01-388 3288

City and Guilds of London Institute
76 Portland Place, London W1N 4AA
01-580 3050

Civil Service Commission
Alencon Link, Basingstoke, Hants RG21 1JB

Institute of Information Scientists
44 Museum Street, London WC1A 1LY
01-831 8003/8633

The Library Association
7 Ridgmount Street, London WC1E 7AE
01-636 7543

The Library Association of Ireland
22 Crofton Road, Dun Laoghaire, Co Dublin, Eire

School Library Association
29-31 George Street, Oxford OX1 2AY
0865 722746

SCONUL (Standing Conference of National and University Libraries)
102 Euston Street, London NW1 2HA
01-387 0317

Important Addresses

Scottish Library Association
Motherwell Business Centre, Coursington Road, Motherwell
0698 52526

Scottish Vocational Education Council (SCOTVEC)
38 Queen Street, Glasgow G1 3DY
041-248 7900

The Society of Archivists
Suffolk Record Office, County Hall, Ipswich IP4 2JS
0473 55801 ext 4232

THE KOGAN PAGE CAREERS SERIES

Written by experts, these practical and useful guides contain detailed information on a wide variety of careers and professions for school-leavers, graduates and people who want to change their present occupation.

Second edition
Careers in Accountancy
Felicity Taylor

Careers in Agriculture & Agricultural Sciences
Susan Black

Careers in Alternative Medicine
Harvey Day

Careers in Antiques
Noël Riley

Careers in Architecture
Oliver Burston

Careers in the Army
Alan S Watts

Fourth edition
Careers in Art and Design
Linda Ball

Careers in Aviation
William Simpson

Third edition
Careers in Banking
Stephen Moss and Julia Allen

Careers in Business
Alan S Watts

Second edition
Careers in Catering and Hotel Management
John S Kinross

Careers in the Church
Judith Taylor

Careers in Civil Engineering
Terry Dennis

Revised edition
Careers in the Civil Service
Peter Medina

Careers in Classical Music
Nella Marcus

Careers in Computing and Information Technology
Eric Deeson

Second edition
Careers in Conservation
John McCormick

Careers in Crafts
Patricia Garnier

Careers in Dance
Jean Richardson

Second edition
Careers in Electrical and Electronic Engineering
Alan S Watts

Third edition
Careers in Engineering
Stephen Moss and Alan S Watts

Careers in Eye Care
*Isobel Fletcher de Tellez
and Robert Fletcher*

Careers in Fashion
Carole Chester

Careers in the Film Industry
Ricki Ostrov

Careers in Floristry and Retail Gardening
Christopher Snook

Third edition
Careers in Hairdressing and Beauty Therapy
Alexa Stace

Careers in the Holiday Industry
Carole Chester

Second edition
Careers in Home Economics
Julie Fish

Careers in Insurance
Jordan Verner

Second edition
Careers in Journalism
Peter Medina

Careers in Land and Property
Judith Huntley

Second edition
Careers in the Law
Elizabeth Usher

Second edition
Careers in Librarianship
Neil Wenborn

Second edition
Careers in Local Government
Felicity Taylor

Third edition
Careers in Marketing, Public Relations and Advertising
Felicity Taylor

Third edition
Careers in Medicine, Dentistry and Mental Health
Judith Humphries

Careers in Modelling
Fleur Hogarth

Careers in Museums and Art Galleries
Neil Wenborn

Revised edition
Careers in the Music Business
Hilary Hayward

Third edition
Careers in Nursing and Allied Professions
Rosemary Clark and Stephen Moss

Careers in Oil and Gas
Philip Algar

Careers in Pharmacy
Werner Tomski

Second edition
Careers in Photography
David Higgs

Second edition
Careers in the Police Force
Jean Joss

Careers in Politics
George Cunningham

Careers in Printing
Colin Cohen

Careers in Psychology
Nedra Du Broff

Careers in Publishing
June Lines

Second edition
Careers in Retailing
Loulou Brown

Careers in Road Transport
David Lewis

Careers at Sea
Alan S Watts

Third edition
Careers in Secretarial and Office Work
Alexa Stace

Third edition
Careers in Social Work
Anne Page

Second edition
Careers in Sport
Chris Middleton

Careers in Surveying
David Crawford

Second edition
Careers in Teaching
Felicity Taylor

Careers in Telecommunications
Felicity Taylor

Careers in Television and Radio
Julia Allen

Second edition
Careers in the Theatre
Jean Richardson

Careers Using Biology
Jenny Willison

Second edition
Careers Using Languages
Helen Steadman

Careers Using Mathematics
Alan S Watts

Careers in Veterinary Surgery
Vivien Donald

Careers Working Abroad
Helen Steadman

Third edition
Careers Working with Animals
Helen Young

Third edition
Careers Working with Children and Young People
Judith Humphries and Julia Allen